AROUND
THE
WORLD

THEN & NOW
By HOWARD GREGORY

Venice

AROUND THE WORLD

THEN & NOW

By HOWARD GREGORY

HOWARD GREGORY ASSOCIATES,   REDONDO BEACH, CALIFORNIA

India

DEDICATED TO MY
BELOVED WIFE JUNE

Rome

THANKS

Rome

"Where did you get the pictures?" is the first thing that most people ask, when they see the beautiful old photographs.

With sincere gratitude, the author would like to acknowledge the assistance received from the following institutions: The Library of Congress; the National Archives; the National Air and Space Museum; the National Art Gallery; the Free Library of Philadelphia; the New York Public Library; the California Historical Society; UCLA; the Academy of Motion Picture Arts and Sciences; the Los Angeles Public Library; the U.S. Navy; the U.S. Air Force and NASA.

He would also like to thank Andrea Wheeler at the Redondo Beach, California Public Library; Peter Collins at the London, England Central Reference Library; Louis S. Deveaud of Paris, France; Helga Bauer of the West Berlin Historical Photo Archives (Bildarchiv Preussiacher Kulturbesitz); Clotilde D'Amato of the Rome Museum (Museo Civilta Romana); Ragi Maher, Inspector of Monuments in Upper Egypt; S.Y. Yim of the Antiquities and Monuments Office in Hong Kong; Li Yuan of Peking (Beijing); Naotake Ito at the National Diet Library in Tokyo; Seikou Komatsu at the Hiroshima Peace Memorial Museum; The Nagasaki International Cultural Hall; the Bishop Museum in Honolulu and the U.S. Navy at Pearl Harbor.

The views of Paris from the UCLA-Special Collections are from the late motion picture actor Charles Boyer's (1899 - 1978) gift of engraved postcard scenes entitled "ANCIEN PARIS" from the 18th and 19th centuries.

Over the years, Hollywood craftsmen have photographed historic scenes in exotic locations all over the world, providing a legacy for future generations. A few of these marvelous scenes are included in the book. Outstanding among these are scenes from Cecil B. DeMille's "The Ten Commandments"; which included the story of the great Egyptian Pharaoh —Ramesses II. The picture was filmed in Egypt with thousands of extras.

The gladiatorial scenes from "Barabbas" are also historical attributes as well as scenes from "A Tale of Two Cities"; "Quo Vadis" and the spectacular chariot race from "Ben Hur." Motion picture studios; museums and other institutions are credited directly in the captions of the pictures.

The spectacular chariot race from the MGM release "BEN HUR" © 1959 Loew's Incorporated. This scene was typical of the Circuses in ancient Rome; there was the Circus Maximus; the Circus Flaminius; Nero's Circus and finally the Circus of Maxentius. There were also amphitheaters such as the Colosseum; the Stadium of Domitian (now the Piazza Navona) and the Castrensian Amphitheatre. The word arena literally meant sand — the floor of the arenas were sand, to soak up the blood of combat. (See Rome Chapter.)

CONTENTS

London

PREFACE

Rome

THEN & NOW photographs tell fascinating stories in the blink of an eye. To see what was once upon a time: alive, vibrant, active people and places as they were and suddenly *tempus fugit* and the contrast between the two photographs conjures instantaneous time travel.

Today the racial melting pot theory is a fact of life in France; Germany; England and America. What about THEN? In the 25th Egyptian Dynasty from 730 to 656 B.C. there were five successive Black Pharaohs, they were Piankhi; Shabaka; Shebitku; Taharqa and Tanutamon (ref. "Encyclopedia Britannica"). Cleopatra (69 to 30 B.C.) was a Macedonian Greek by origin and more probably blonde than brunette (ref. Will Durant's, "Story of Civilization"). The Huns (Asiatic barbarians) devastated and controlled Europe under Attila in the 5th century A.D. However, these are only highlights and as Alexander Pope (1688-1744) said, "A little learning is a dangerous thing". Conversely, the next line (from An Essay on Criticism) is the least known and the most significant: "Drink deep, or taste not the Pierian spring..." The primary bibliographical sources are "The Encyclopedia Britannica", "The National Geographic" and Will Durant's "The Story of Civilization", as well as those books indicated directly in the captions.

A small percentage of the NOW photos in this book are from NASA; U.S. Air Force; U.S. Navy, etc. and credit for these are noted directly in the captions. Unless noted otherwise in the captions, all of the other NOW photos around the world were taken by the author, Howard Gregory.

Published by
HOWARD GREGORY ASSOCIATES
640 The Village #209
Redondo Beach, California 90277

International Standard Book Number (ISBN) 0-9607086-2-6 (Softbound Edition)
International Standard Book Number (ISBN) 0-9607086-3-4 (Hardcover Edition)
Library of Congress Catalog Card Number   85-90964

First Printing 1986

THIS BOOK IS AVAILABLE FROM YOUR LOCAL BOOKSTORE.
THE BOOK IS ALSO AVAILABLE BY MAIL ORDER FROM:

HOWARD GREGORY
640 THE VILLAGE #209
REDONDO BEACH, CALIFORNIA 90277

Other books by Howard Gregory: "The Falcon's Disciples";
"Parachuting's Unforgettable Jumps";
"Southern California's Seacoast THEN & NOW"

PRINTED IN THE UNITED STATES OF AMERICA
By Delta Lithograph • Van Nuys, CA

COVER: Engraving from Charles Nordoff's, "Northern California, Oregon and the Sandwich Islands," published in 1874. Photo of Hula girls at the famous Kodak Hula Show at Waikiki Beach.

Paris when it drizzles.

THE ADVENTURES OF A GLOBETROTTER

HE supreme joy of being writer; photographer; editor and publisher is that you can do it your way. And as that old baseball great Dizzy Dean once said, "If you don't toot your own horn — nobody is going to toot it for you!"

It took a couple of years of research to gather up the classic old photographs from around the world and all of these sources are listed elsewhere in the book. Counting the five cities in the United States, it took about a year to find all the unique locations in the old photos and shoot those pictures. Many of the pictures took real detective work to find the precise spot.

The Nile

My beloved wife, June, died suddenly from cancer — caused by cigarettes. We had been to Europe and the Middle East a few times and had shot a few of the pictures. One of the highlights of our life was a 17 day cruise on the Golden Odyssey: Athens; Cairo; the Holy Land; Istanbul; Delphi and the Greek Islands. This was travelling in style, to out of the ordinary places and it is a wonderful, happy memory.

The travel on the around the world trip was by plane; train; bus; taxi; helicopter; cruise ship; ferry boat; camel; elephant and the most walking since the Infantry in World War II.

LONDON: The classic old photo at the foot of Ludgate hill in 1902 features a Bobby (London Policeman) and there wasn't a Bobby in sight. At Old Bailey (the Police Headquarters) the Officer on duty actually assigned Constable Chris Corke to pose for the picture. The whole thing only took about ten minutes; but it was typical of the British hospitality and good manners.

The Vecchio Bridge — Florence

The Forbidden City in Peking (Beijing)

PARIS: You hear snobs say, "When I go to Paris I'm going to go to the places the tourists don't go."

Well if you do, you are going to miss the Arch of Triumph; the Champs Elysees; the Eiffel Tower; the Louvre; Notre Dame; Montmartre and it about leaves you with the sewer and the jail.

The Paris subway will take you to almost anyplace in Paris; it's the only way to travel in Paris.

BERLIN: There is something good about the Berlin Wall and that is it exposes the Soviet tyranny for the evil empire that it is. The subversive writers in the media, TV, etc., can rationalize all they want — hinting that Russia is no Boogey Man and they're not out to conquer anybody and the two super-powers, the Soviet Union and the U.S.A. both have their faults; but they are all lies. Because the Iron Curtain, coined by Winston Churchill, is a stark reality in Berlin, where 73 refugees have been killed trying to cross to freedom at the Berlin Wall.

Going past the famous "Check Point Charlie" to East Berlin was a depressing experience. The difference between the freedom of West Berlin versus East Berlin was like day and night. In West Berlin at the bustling Plaza adjacent to the Wilhelm Memorial Church, teen-age boys costumed in black leather, with chains hanging around their neck and weird punk haircuts were actually comic in appearance. There weren't any motorcycles in sight, they would have completed the picture; people giggled looking at them in the freedom of West Berlin. I doubt very much if these comic punkers' freedom would have been tolerated in East Berlin.

Egypt

THE ADVENTURES OF A GLOBETROTTER

SWITZERLAND: The Matterhorn; Rifflehorn; Zermatt Triangle, in this writer's opinion, is the most beautiful area in the world. Of course, there is an area in California that gives it very stiff competition every spring and early summer when the snows of the High Sierra's are melting and the falls are flowing and that is the Yosemite Valley.

VENICE: An artist's and photographer's dream. It is the most beautiful city in the world. Of course, beauty is in the eyes of the beholder. Some people only see trash floating in a canal or rust and decay and they love to say how Venice is continually sinking into the Mediterranean Sea. It's like the poem, "Two men look out through the bars; One sees the mud, and one sees the stars." F. Langbridge, (A Cluster of Quiet Thoughts).

ROME: This guy in the bus station, adjacent to the railroad station in Central Rome spoke better English than I did; he was showing me what bus to catch to get to the Museum on the outskirts of Rome where they have a complete model of Ancient Rome. The bus was Number 93 — I won't forget it. Then he insisted that I hurry and get my ticket; he pushed me in front of the ticket line. I paid for the ticket and when I went to put the change back in my wallet I couldn't find it. I was in shock. I looked around and my smooth talking buddy was also gone; he had disappeared into thin air and I was standing there like the Hill Billy that had just been taken by the city slicker.

My wallet contained some cash, traveler's checks and driver's license — which I could do without. But my credit card was also in the wallet.

The Rome Police Station was jammed with men and women (mostly women) filling out lengthy reports in quadruplicate. It was an epidemic like the Black Plague; I wasn't alone. You always feel it can't happen to you — but it can, believe me.

Then I remembered the magician at the Stardust in Las Vegas and how he came down off the stage, wandered through the audience, shaking hands and hugging people, Then he went back to the stage and unloaded his pockets onto a table.

He had wallets, wrist watches, purses, and all kinds of comical items he had taken from people (like suspenders and a brassiere). The victims all came up on stage and claimed their items and the magician got a big hand. I believe that guy is now working Rome.

As a postscript: Reports from the credit card people show that Slippery Sam is travelling all over Italy having a ball with the credit card.

The Rome Museum (Museo Della Civilto Romana) was closed for repairs. I banged on the door and through charades and my broken Italian explained that I was a writer and would like to see the model of Ancient Rome.

Miss D'Amato a pretty archeologist at the Museum let me into the huge main hall where the fabulous model is located. I was anxious to verify the location of Nero's Circus; because I had read that it was located where Saint Peter's (the largest church in the world) is located today. I was thrilled to see where it was located and what it actually looked like. And I was allowed to photograph it.

The fabulous picture of the "Temple of Venus" with the Arch of Titus, thanks to Miss D'Amato, was also a great addition to the book, as well as the other artistic pictures of the model.

ATHENS: The French call it, "Deja Vu"; as if you'd been there before. The Parthenon inspired that sensation like a homecoming. I truly believe that my ancestors were there at that spot. And I also believe that the Parthenon during the Golden Age of Greece was the most beautiful building in the world — in any age.

In the major cities in the United States you can take a helicopter ride for between $25 and $50 and you don't need anybodies' signature. And for my previous book "Southern California's Seacoast THEN and NOW," the Goodyear Blimp "Columbia" was gracious enough to be my camera-platform free; plus I could bring along two guests; plus for the thrill of a lifetime I piloted the "Columbia" for 30 minutes of our two hour flight.

THEN & NOW

California

Berlin

THE ADVENTURES OF A GLOBETROTTER

Not so in Europe; there, they want an arm and a leg; plus the signature of God. In Athens, on the news-stands, I noticed a superb picture book on "ATHENS" with a great cover shot of the Acropolis. The publisher (Ekdotike Athenon S.A.) agreed — at a nominal fee — to let me use their great picture in the book. I was thrilled.

EGYPT: "Look! You've got your Indiana Jones' hat on," my son, Buzz snickered at the Egyptian pictures.

"I wore that hat to protect my bean from the scorching desert sun," I smiled, "and I wore a hat like that before Indiana Jones was born."

Egypt was the highlight of my "Around the World" (in would you believe 80 days?) trip. Abu Simbel can use all the Hollywood adjectives like — Fabulous; Colossal or Sensational. And Abu Simbel is a must for any trip to the Upper Nile.

Don't be fooled, the Upper Nile actually means nearly a thousand miles south of the Mediterranean in Nubia, because the Nile flows from there and it also gets quite warm there.

The Upper Nile cruise to Luxor; Karnak; The Valley of the Kings and all the numerous Temples along the Nile was an unforgettable adventure.

Luck has a great deal to do with the art of taking good pictures and I was very lucky on the cruise of the Upper Nile to have two beautiful women who were willing to pose for me and I was delighted with the results.

Helen Flaherty from Australia posed exactly like the French yacht-women from 1894 and in the same type wicker chair. However, a random profile shot taken while we were sailing in a felucca on the Nile had so much pizzazz that that picture was used instead.

Adrienne Niedersuss from Austria had all the attributes of a Vogue model in her sexy attire with the Nile in the background.

The highlight of the trip Around the World was having my very own camel for two days and trotting all over the Giza Desert, taking photos of the Sphinx and Pyramids. I'd go all the way out to the horizon in the desert and shoot back at different angles.

My guide was "Jimmy Carter" (real name — Gamal Fekrey El Gabry), my camel "Cha Cha Cha" and his donkey was called, "Cholly Brown." Jimmy speaks excellent English and he is a very funny young man. Trotting along, he would start singing, "The camels are coming — tra la, tra la!" and saying all kinds of comical phrases that he obviously picked up from American teenagers. Guide Jimmy Carter usually hangs out around the Sphinx and he is highly recommended.

Queen Nefertiti's bust (her head dummy) in the Berlin Museum was exquisite. Surprisingly, her skin color, which looked very natural, was very fair, as an example — like Marilyn Monroe and the super fine detail of the bust leads you to believe that this actually was the true skin texture of Queen Nefertiti.

Ironically, drawings, paintings and artwork for sale to the tourists in Egypt portray Queen Nefertiti as being black. I'll probably be accused of being a racist for making a statement like that — but it's true.

THE HOLY LAND: To actually walk where Jesus walked in the Holy Land is an emotional experience visiting the River Jordan; Bethlehem; Nazareth and Jerusalem.

The Dark Ages when the Barbarians over-ran Europe set civilization back a thousand years and that is the time span between the awesome dome on Santa Sophia in Istanbul (Constantinople) and the dome on Saint Peter's in Rome. Apparently through the Dark Ages they forgot how to construct those colossal domes until Michelangelo designed the dome for Saint Peter's.

THE TAJ MAHAL: For centuries the Taj Mahal in India has been called, "The Most Beautiful Building in the World." After seeing and photographing it from many angles, I concur; or as Howard Cosell might say, "I indubitably acquiesce."

Riding on top of an elephant in India was fun. Also watching the quick reflexes of a mongoose and a cobra while the snake charmer played his flute was unusual curb-side entertainment.

HONG KONG: After the dust and heat of Egypt and India, Hong Kong was a very pleasant surprise; a very modern city with elegant high-rises, huge, classy air-conditioned shopping arcades, where the prices are reasonable.

The Ferry ride from Hong Kong to Kowloon on the mainland for pennies is a treat that should not be missed.

I felt like Sam Spade looking for the "Maltese Falcon" trying to locate the hotel where the exterior shots were made for the movie, "The World of Suzie Wong." I wanted to include it in the Hong Kong chapter of the book.

The first day in Hong Kong I asked the pretty girl at the desk, "Could you please tell me where the hotel is where they shot "The World of Suzie Wong?"

She looked at me as if to say, "You dirty old man," and she said that there were lots of those kind of bars, right over on the next street.

THEN & NOW

Hollywood   India

THE ADVENTURES OF A GLOBETROTTER

Hollywood

THEN & NOW

Egypt

Everyone thought I wanted to get laid. I asked cab drivers and they would say, "Oh, sure I know where it is," and I was convinced that I finally found the hotel. And we would wind up at the local girlie establishment.

Finally, I really convinced a guy that I was a writer-photographer working on a book and he believed me. And best of all, he knew where it was located. He drew a map and gave me directions. After trudging all over the hill, I finally located the intersection up on the side of the hill. From the notoriety of the movie, the street had been renamed "Hollywood Road". The old hotel in the movie was now a Curio Shop. Time marches on.

Hong Kong is a great city for travellers; a city of entrepreneurs; beautiful women and friendly people.

PEKING (BEIJING): Flying across China for 1,200 miles from Hong Kong to Peking was unusual. The reason is — I've flown from coast to coast (3,000 miles) across the United States dozens of times and every state has vast areas that were unpopulated; some states in the west these areas extended for hundreds of miles. Not so in China; flying from Hong Kong to Peking was a solid quilt of neat farms. 1.1 billion people.

The Great Wall Hotel in Peking was my most expensive hotel, but it was also the very best. The United States could never have a hotel that could even equal the Great Wall Hotel. It is an elegant hotel with a great many attributes that could be duplicated in the U.S. except two.

The first reason is that the waitresses and clerks are very pretty *"slender"* young girls between 18 and 22 years old (I know because I asked them) who speak English.

Now I ask you, would the Women's Libbers and the ACLU sit still for this in the U.S.? You bet your bippy they wouldn't; all the fatties, uglies and oldies would be screaming discriminations. And the courts have already ruled that the fatties win.

And the second reason is because both the Chinese young women and the few young men at the Great Wall Hotel are dedicated, happy, smiling employees who enjoy their work. (Or at least they convincingly act like they do.) Now, could this happen in unionized America?

The hotel also has many other features e.g. indoor pool; classical piano; beautiful architecture, etc.

The Great Wall of China was truly an unexpectedly amazing trip. It was much more than I had anticipated. And Yuan, my pretty Chinese guide, who volunteered at the hotel for the equivalent of $18, made it much more enjoyable.

It was a two hour drive, one way to the Great Wall from Peking. After climbing all over the wall at Pa-Ta-Ling we returned to Peking to visit the Forbidden City, a national shrine for the Chinese people. The grandeur of its ancient temples and pavilions draw thousands of people from all over China.

Peking had numerous motorcycles with side-cars; I kept thinking of Hollywood stuntmen and anticipated the guy on the bike to do his thing. Peking also had many Chinese families (only one child per family allowed) from out of town visiting the shrines; hordes of bicycles; tree lined streets; a pleasant climate and a polite, congenial, proud people.

SHANGHAI: 12,000,000 people live in Shanghai, the gateway to the Yangtze (Changjiang) River basin. Chinese from the inland provinces love to walk the waterfront along the Huangpu River bank, formerly called the Bund (Zhongshan Dong Z-LU), to watch the ships and take river excursions. It was apparent that I was the first foreigner or American that many of them had ever seen in person and they would stare and point at me. At first I thought maybe my fly was open. They were extremely friendly. One young man touched the skin on my hand, smiling.

I bought a colorful Chinese ceramic horse in Shanghai that I treasure and it was very inexpensive. The shopping in Shanghai was a true bargain.

TOKYO: The subway in Tokyo equals that of Paris when it comes to blanketing the entire city. And like Paris — no graffiti and most of the people are dressed, i.e. most men wear ties and jackets and the women wear dresses.

Tokyo's recovery from the devastations of World War II like Berlin's recovery has been phenomenal. In the crowded downtown areas the only oddball looking people are usually American.

NAGASAKI: I see this big truck drive by and incredibly, instead of watching where he is going, the guy is eating his breakfast out of a cup with chopsticks. Holy Mackerel! For me just to eat with chopsticks is pretty tricky — but, no hands for the truck? Then I realize that in Japan they drive on the left like the British and he wasn't really driving, the guy on his right was.

The domestic airlines in Japan were superior to any I'd flown before

THE ADVENTURES OF A GLOBETROTTER

and one of the outstanding features was a TV camera mounted under the fuselage of the plane that projected an excellent large picture onto the motion picture screen in the cabin.

The passengers could actually see how the plane taxied around the airport; taking off and landing as well as some vertical in-flight pictures. The unique feature of this added entertainment was that it was live and happening while you were watching it. The take-offs and especially the landings were equal or better than any of the shows at Tokyo's Disneyland, which is also highly recommended.

Baseball is big in Japan and at all ages; just like in the United States. The teams have all the usual names, like "The Lions" and "The Tigers".

I saw one little league boy in his uniform and his team was different — he was a proud player on "The Dragons".

HAWAII: It was my first trip to Hawaii and Waikiki Beach. Practically everyone I talked to had bad-mouthed Waikiki Beach saying, "Don't go to Waikiki — go to Whatsisname."

But I had classic old pictures of Honolulu and Waikiki Beach — I had to go there. I had expected to find another Santa Monica.

Was I surprised! Don't believe what people say — because the beach of Waikiki is now my favorite of the entire world. Catamarans; outrigger canoes and dolphins leaping out of the water and snorkeling and taking underwater pictures with inexpensive rented equipment.

I needed some pictures of girls in bikinis for contrast to the old times in the classic old photos of Waikiki. So, I had to become a true live "Bikini Inspector." For real. Scouts honor. I'd show an advertisement handout for my previous book and explain that I'd like to take their picture. And they'd look down their nose as if to say get lost. And I wasn't wearing my trench coat or I could have flashed them.

Anyhow, I wound up by saying, "I'll give you ten dollars, to let me take your picture and I'll mail you a copy of the book." That worked.

Meanwhile, back at the beach. Let's get back to the "Bikini Inspector" part. All men are voyeurs to a certain degree, because that is part of human nature. Getting to the Waikiki early and getting a good spot in the back, with good visibility is important. Most girls wear bikinis, but they arrive at the beach wearing shorts and blouses over the bikinis. The fun part is watching them remove their shorts and blouses.

Some are timid and shy, while others flaunt their attributes. Some sit down and slither out of their clothes and with others you can almost hear the music blaring, "Take it off! Take it all off!" as they go through their ritual.

I needed three girls for the picture, so for a superior picture the ideal would be 3 tens; of course 2 tens and nine would be OK. The way my luck was running I'd be lucky to get 3 sevens. After about an hour of official bikini inspecting the field was narrowed down. Out of a hundred or so people in the area there were about 6 nines, who might be tens if they could pose.

I planned my attack. The first two turned sour. And the next two — Bingo — OK. After that, number three was easy. All three were eighteen years old; blondes and slender. So far so good.

I gave each of the girls a lei of flowers for around her neck to give the picture a holiday atmosphere. They giggled and started to act stupid. After they settled down we shot some pictures. Pleased with the results, I told the girls to keep the leis; gave them each ten dollars and had them sign a release so I could use the picture for publication.

The payoff was, the girls in the bikinis were pretty in the pictures, but I couldn't use them because they were all posed slightly different and that contrasts poorly to Hawaiian Hula girls. Luckily the Kodak Hula Show saved the day and I got good pictures where the girls are all in perfect unison.

I can't say enough about the beauty of Waikiki Beach; the water was a beautiful emerald green and you can swim out 300 yards and stand up, with the water up to your waist. They call Hawaii "Paradise" and that's good enough for me.

Howard Gregory, was Light-heavyweight Boxing Champion of the 504th Parachute Infantry Regiment (1942). After the war, he worked extra, bits and did a few stunts, working all the major studios in Hollywood. He made his first parachute jump in June, '1942 and took up skydiving in March 1964 and he wrote two successful books on parachuting. He also was an analyst in the aircraft industry from which he is now retired.

THEN & NOW

Philadelphia (1941)   *Egypt*

London

From King Arthur to the Beatles

15

THEN & NOW:

Above, the Tower of London in the Seventeenth Century. (Courtesy of the Library of Congress.) The Tower is the most famous monument in the British Isles. On Christmas 1066 William I built fortifications here. It has held many notable prisoners including Elizabeth I and Sir Walter Raleigh. Rudolph Hess was the last notable prisoner in 1941. Many motion-pictures have been made about the atrocities, executions and infamous murders that took place in the Tower. In 1381 the Archbishop of Canterbury was dragged out of St. John's Chapel by Wat Tyler's men and beheaded. On May 21, 1471 King Henry VI was murdered there. The two young nephews of Richard III were murdered there in August 1483. Two of Henry VIII's wives, Anne Boleyn (1536) and Catherine Howard (1542) were executed there; as was Sir Thomas More (1535) and Lady Jane Grey (1554). Until the reign of James I, the Tower was a royal residence as well as the mint, the public records, the ordnance store and the royal menagerie. To-day a military garrison still occupies the barracks in the Tower seen below and presently the Crown Jewels are kept there.

THEN & NOW: ABOVE: Stonehenge on the Salisbury Plains in Southern England was built over a 400 year period between 1900 BC and 1500 BC — long before Rome itself was founded. It was a sophisticated and intelligently conceived astronomical observatory in which extreme positions of the sun and moon were aligned to significant stones. BELOW: At one time the largest steerable parabolic dish antenna in the world; located at Jodrell Bank in England. The 250 foot radio mirror is used to eavesdrop on deep space as well as track space-craft. (Courtesy of the National Archives.) OPPOSITE PAGE TOP: London in 1620 from an engraving by J. Visscher. Notice the skulls stuck on the ends of the pikes over the entrance to Old London Bridge, which was built in 1209 and survived for 600 years, with its tunnel-like street of houses and shops. It was the only road between the north and south sides of London. Business and merchants were in the north; the south contrasted with theatres, taverns, brothels and jails. In the foreground is the famous Southwark Cathedral. OPPOSITE PAGE BOTTOM: The Southwark Cathedral is on the left and the bridge is half hidden behind the high-rise on the right. (Old London drawing courtesy of the National Archives.)

NOTE: Shakespeare worshipped at Southwark Cathedral and his famous Globe Theatre was close by.

THEN & NOW: ABOVE: The Royal Exchange in London, early in the Nineteenth Century (Courtesy of the Library of Congress.) BELOW: The same scene today. OPPOSITE PAGE TOP: Regent Street in London at the turn of the century. (Courtesy of the Library of Congress.) OPPOSITE PAGE BOTTOM: The exact same location today. 202 Regent seen on the awning, above left, is to the left of the automobile by the curb.

REGENT STREET LONDON. 534b. J.V.

THEN & NOW: Above, London, England — Westminster Abbey, Westminster Hall and the first Parliament in 1647. (Courtesy of the New York Public Library.) Below, the same scene today.

THEN & NOW: Above, London, England at King's Cross in 1901. (Courtesy of the National Archives.)
Below, today.

21

THEN & NOW:

ABOVE: London in 1896 at St. Martin-le Grand. The Post Office building with the columns was demolished in 1910. (Courtesy of the Free Library of Philadelphia.) BELOW: That same location; the building that was the Post Office is today St. Martin's House for brokers and attorneys. OPPOSITE PAGE TOP: London at Holborn looking east in 1895. (Courtesy of the Free Library of Philadelphia.) OPPOSITE PAGE BOTTOM: The same exact location today. Notice the same building on the right in both pictures. Also a double-decker bus dominates both pictures.

THEATRE ROYAL, COVENT GARDEN.

Published Jan.y 12, 1828, by Jones & Co. 3 Acton Place, Kingsland Road, London.

24

THEN & NOW:

ABOVE: "The Royal Covent Garden Theatre" in London. Engraving by John Rolph published January 12, 1828. (Courtesy of the Library of Congress.) BELOW: Today it is called "The Royal Opera House" and they present operas such as, "The Barber of Seville" and "La Boheme"; and ballets such as, "Swan Lake" and "Sleeping Beauty." OPPOSITE PAGE TOP: The bridge at the bottom of Ludgate Hill in 1902. (Courtesy of the National Archives.) OPPOSITE PAGE BOTTOM: London Policeman, Chris Corke, was kind enough to pose in the same spot as Policeman in the above photograph.

THEN & NOW: ABOVE: The famous Piccadilly Circus in London, early in the Twentieth Century. (Courtesy of the Los Angeles Public Library.) BELOW: Today. OPPOSITE PAGE TOP: The Oxford Street Pantheon built in 1772. Drawn by J. Hinchliff. (Courtesy of the Library of Congress.) OPPOSITE PAGE BOTTOM: The Pantheon is now the Academy Cinema Theater (same location) in the Soho District of London.

Drawn by Tho. H. Shepherd.
Engraved by J. Hinchliff.

PANTHEON, OXFORD ST.

THEN & NOW:

Below, Saint Paul's Cathedral, London, England in 1941 at the corner of Warwick Lane and Paternoster Row. Whole sections of the street system were obliterated during the war. More than 30,000 were killed and 50,000 injured. (Courtesy of the Library of Congress.) Above, that same location today.

THEN & NOW: Above, a World War I Bomber — the English Handley-Page aircraft, just prior to a bombing mission on August 9, 1918. Below, Great Britain's Panavia Tornado has a maximum speed of 1,452 mph — Mach 2.2 at 36,000 ft. Its armaments consist of many types of nuclear and conventional weapons including two built-in 27 mm Mauser cannons. (Photos courtesy of the National Air and Space Museum).

Paris

C'est Magnifique

71 — ANCIEN PARIS. — Plâtrières Clignancourt, versant est de la Butte Montmartre vers 1830.

THEN & NOW: ABOVE: The Montmartre in Paris in 1830. BELOW: The Moulin Rouge in the Montmartre today. OPPOSITE PAGE TOP: The Montmartre in 1850. OPPOSITE PAGE BOTTOM: A classic Parisian street scene. Paris when it drizzles. Crowning the heights of the Montmartre is the dome of Sacre-Coeur which can be seen from nearly every part of Paris. (Dwgs. courtesy of UCLA.)

73 — ANCIEN PARIS. — La Butte Montmartre en 1850. *ND Phot*.

Autre vue Particuliere de Paris depuis Nôtre Dame jusques au Pont de la Tournelle,
où l'on voit dans l'alignement l'hôtel de Ville, S! Jean en Greve, S! Gervais, & le pont Rouge, prise du Quay de Miramion.

433. — ANCIEN PARIS.   Vue sur la Seine sous Louis XV.
Dessin et gravure de J. Rigaud.   ND Phot.

THEN & NOW: ABOVE: Paris at the Seine River with Notre Dame Cathedral in the 18th Century. Notre Dame was begun in 1163 but was not completed for 100 years. It is located on an island in the Seine called La Cite. Picture courtesy of UCLA Special Collections — from the collection of the late motion picture actor Charles Boyer; nine of this Paris collection are included in this book (with black borders.) BELOW: The same scene today. OPPOSITE PAGE TOP: Notre Dame and the Seine River in 1765. OPPOSITE PAGE BELOW: Today.

32

335 — ANCIEN PARIS. — Vue de Notre-Dame, de l'Archevêché, du Pont Notre-Dame et du Quai des Bernardins, vers 1765. (D'après Lallemand.) ND Phot.

205 — ANCIEN PARIS. — Le Pont de Saint-Cloud vers 1805. *ND Phot.*

THEN & NOW: ABOVE: Saint Cloud Bridge in 1805. BELOW: The Saint Cloud Bridge today. OPPOSITE PAGE TOP: The Arcole Bridge in the 19th Century with ice-skaters frolicking on the Seine. OPPOSITE PAGE BOTTOM: That same location today. (Dwgs. courtesy of UCLA.)

312 — ANCIEN PARIS. — La Grande Joute des Mariniers, entre le Pont au Change et le Pont Notre-Dame, la Pompe Notre-Dame (1751), d'après Raguenet.   *ND Phot.*

THEN & NOW:

ABOVE: The Pont au Change (Bridge) where the money changers opened their shops by order of Louis VII in 1141. In 1647 the bridge was rebuilt with five-story stone houses on each side. BELOW: The same scene today. The bridge actually was located between these two bridges about where the boat is located. OPPOSITE PAGE TOP: The Louvre in 1752. OPPOSITE PAGE BOTTOM: The Louvre today. In 1793 the King's Royal Palace became the Louvre Museum and today it is the world's greatest treasury of art, with 50 galleries and 3,000 masterpiece paintings, including the incomparable Mona Lisa by Leonardo da Vinci. French giants, Jean-Baptiste Chardin and Jacques-Louis David, as well as Rembrandt Cellini and Michelangelo are also represented. The Venus de Milo and the Winged Victory of Samothrace, two classic Greek beauties that were created before Christ are the crowning glories of this monumental palace, that requires eight miles of walking to go through all the rooms. (Dwgs. courtesy of UCLA.)

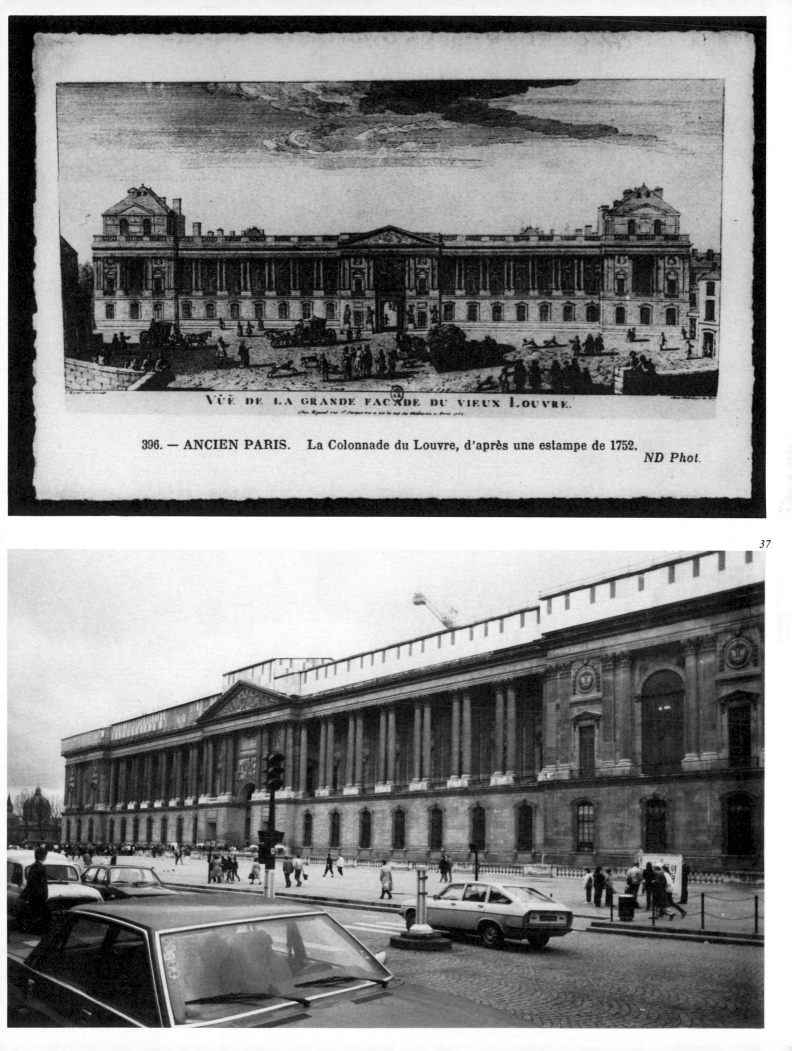

VÜE DE LA GRANDE FACADE DU VIEUX LOUVRE.

396. — ANCIEN PARIS. La Colonnade du Louvre, d'après une estampe de 1752.

ND Phot.

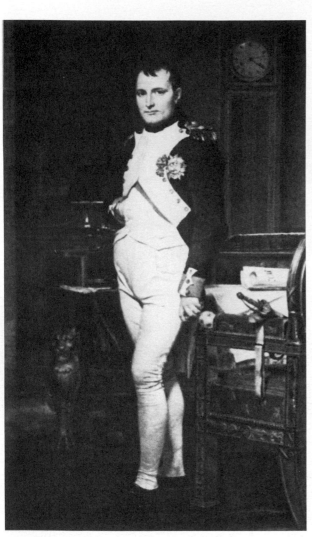

THEN & NOW:

ABOVE LEFT: Napoleon (1769 - 1821), Emperor of France from 1804 to 1814 and again for "The Hundred Days" in 1815 (Picture courtesy of the National Gallery of Art in Washington, D.C.; titled "Napoleon in his study, 1812" by Jacques—Louis David (1748 - 1825). Napoleon Bonaparte has been called genius, opportunist, intelligent and tyrant. Through exceptional skill and political allies he rose through the ranks of the military. He had indignantly witnessed the terror of the mob during the Revolution. At age 30 he imposed a military dictatorship on France (1799). In 1802 a national hero, he was elected consul for life by an overwhelming majority of 3,500,000 votes to less than 10,000. Napoleon left many durable institutions, such as the Napoleonic Code, which gave permanent form to the great gains of the Revolution, individual liberty and equality before the law. He also instituted the Banque de France, the financial organizations, the university and the military academies. For France and the world he was a hero for an age. Napoleon's three greatest achievements were: Peace in Europe; the appeasement of the church (The Concordat) and his life consulship. At his coronation as emperor at Notre Dame on December 2, 1804, he took the crown from the Pope's hands and set it on his own head himself. TOP OF PAGE: Napoleon's tomb. CENTER OF PAGE: The Arch of Triumph. Napoleon ordered the building of it in 1806; it was completed in 1836. OPPOSITE PAGE TOP: Looking down the famous Champs Elysees toward the Arch of Triumph in the early 1800's. (Dwg. courtesy of UCLA.) OPPOSITE PAGE BOTTOM: The same scene today.

NOTE: The peace in Europe noted above was "The Peace of Amiens" on March 25, 1802 which led to Napoleon's landslide election to consul for life in August, 1802. The later Napoleonic Wars (1804-15) would cost France itself 500,000 of its young men; a horrifying price to pay for the gains noted above.

470. — ANCIEN PARIS.   Les Champs-Elysées sous Louis-Philippe, projet de Couronnement de l'Arc de Triomphe, par Barye.   *ND Phot.*

40

THEN & NOW:

ABOVE: Winston Churchill (1874 - 1965) and Charles de Gaulle (1890 - 1970) parade victoriously down the Champs Elysees on November 11, 1944 during World War II. It was Churchill's first visit to liberated Paris. (That date was also the 26th Anniversary to the end of World War I.) Notice the people on top of the Arch of Triumph which rises 160 feet above the Place de l'Etoile (the star) so named because 12 avenues radiate from it like the points of a star. The view from the top presents an excellent panorama of Paris (Courtesy of the National Archives.) BELOW: The Arch of Triumph today. OPPOSITE PAGE TOP: The interior of Notre Dame Cathedral from the TABLEAUX DE PARIS PENDANT LA REVOLUTION FRANCAISE 1789 - 1792. Published in 1902 by Pierre de Nolhac. (Courtesy of UCLA.) OPPOSITE PAGE BOTTOM: Notre Dame today.

THEN & NOW:

ABOVE: The Eiffel Tower under construction in 1888 photograph by Pierre Petit. (Courtesy of National Archives.) The Eiffel Tower was completed for **the** 1889 World's Fair celebrating the 100th anniversary of the French Revolution; it was built by France's famous structural engineer, Alexandre Gustave Eiffel (1832 - 1923) who also built bridges as well as the framework for the Statue of Liberty. At 984 feet it was at that time the tallest structure in the world. The renown landmark has gourmet restaurants, cafes, displays and even a small theatre. BELOW: The Eiffel Tower today. OPPOSITE PAGE TOP: Celebrating the Revolution from TABLEAUX DE PARIS PENDANT LA REVOLUTION FRANCAISE 1789 - 1792. Published in 1902 by Pierre de Holfac. (Courtesy of UCLA.) The Arch was a wooden structure erected for the celebration of July 14, 1790; the first anniversary of the storming of the Bastille (it was dismantled after the celebration.) OPPOSITE PAGE BELOW: Today at the same location as the wooden arch sits the Eiffel Tower.

THEN & NOW: ABOVE: Paris in 1635. A view of Pont Neuf by Jacques Callot (1592 - 1635). (Courtesy of UCLA.) BELOW: The same scene today. OPPOSITE PAGE TOP: The guillotine scene from the MGM release "A TALE OF TWO CITIES" © 1935 Metro-Goldwyn-Mayer Corporation. (Renewed 1962 Metro-Goldwyn-Mayer Inc.) Historically it was January 21, 1793 when King Louis XVI was taken to his execution at the Place de la Revolution. He attempted to plead his innocence to the crowd; but the signal was given and the rolling of the drums drowned him out. And the blade fell. OPPOSITE PAGE BOTTOM: The Place de la Revolution is today the Place de la Concorde.

44

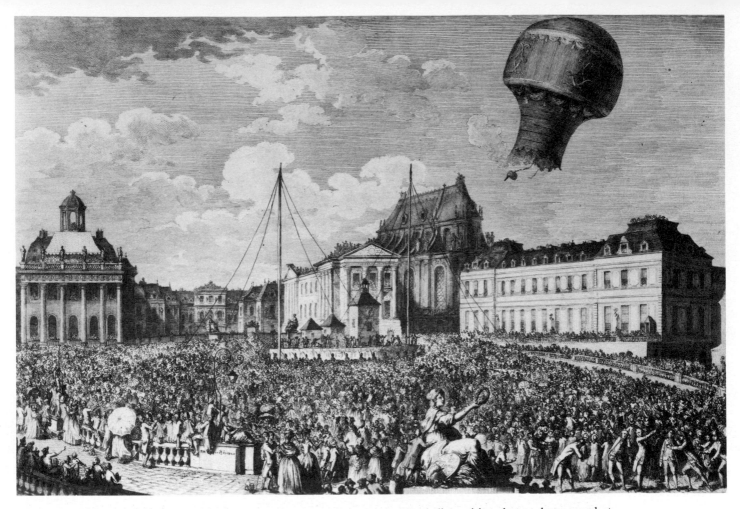

THEN & NOW: Above, An artist's concept shows the Montgolfier balloon rising above a huge crowd at Versailles, France on September 19, 1783 sending a sheep, a rooster and a duck aloft as passengers. On November 21, 1783 the Montgolfier brothers, Joseph (1740 - 1810) and Jacques (1745 - 1799), sent up the first manned free flight. The balloon sailed for 5½ miles over Paris in 25 minutes. The two brothers were honored by the French Academie des Sciences for their work. (Library of Congress.) Below, An artist's concept shows Voyager 1 spacecraft as it flew by Jupiter on March 5, 1979, Voyager 2 followed on July 9. The Voyager spacecraft sent back exceptional photographs of Jupiter and her moons with volcanic activity: Europa with ice and rock; Ganymede dotted with impact craters and Callisto cratered and covered with ice. (NASA)

46

47

THEN & NOW: Above, Louis Bleriot making his epoch-making flight across the English Channel on July 25, 1909. Flying his own Bleriot XI Monoplane from Calais to Dover, he won a 4,000 franc prize. Below, an Air France Concorde, the world's first supersonic passenger aircraft which makes daily 3½ hour flights from New York to Paris. West bound flights are really fast — you get there 2½ hours before you left — e.g. they depart Paris at 11 AM and arrive in New York at 8:30 AM; beating the sun by 2½ hours. (Above, National Air and Space Museum; Below, Air France.)

48

Berlin

The Romance of the Red Baron Lives

49

THEN & NOW:

Above, Berlin, Germany at the turn of the century. The statue of "Berolina" was erected in 1895. Across the Alexanderplatz is the famous Grand Hotel. Hollywood in 1932 glamorized this hotel with an all-star cast including Lionel Barrymore, John Barrymore, Greta Garbo, Joan Crawford, Wallace Beery and Lewis Stone. "Grand Hotel" won the Academy Award for best picture in 1932 and over fifty years later it can still be viewed with pleasure. The 1959 German remake was titled, "Menschen im Hotel." Today MGM's palatial hotel in Las Vegas is fittingly named the Grand Hotel. (Courtesy of the National Archives.) Below, the Alexanderplatz today in East Berlin. The Television tower's globe contains a restaurant with a view of all Berlin.

50

THEN & NOW:

ABOVE: The Ace of Aces of World War I was Baron Manfred von Richthofen (1892 - 1918) with 80 victories. The legendary "Red Baron" flew his red Fokker Triplane above his "Flying Circus" of Fokker D7 biplanes. Compared to the mud, agony and terror of the trench warfare below, their's was a glorious, adventurous battle in the skies; comparable to knighthood in its flower. The fight was clean, quick and open. The "Red Knight of Germany" developed three and four plane formation flying which dominated the Allied pilots. Soon the Allies were also flying formations and Richthofen would dive out of the sun from above. His leadership, flying skill and superior German aircraft made him a legend during his own lifetime, which was short. Canadian Captain Roy Brown was credited with shooting down the Baron when he was flying dangerously close to the ground. However, the excellent book, "Fighter Aces", by Colonel Raymond F. Toliver and Trevor Constable pretty well proves that the Baron's death was caused by ground fire. At only 150 feet altitude the tiny red Fokker banked and turned for the German side of the front lines, side slipping into a rise that ripped off the landing gear bringing the Triplane to a screeching halt. A single bullet had entered the chest. The Red Baron was buried by the Allies at Bertangles with full military honors, including a firing squad and a guard of honor consisting of six captains. (National Air and Space Museum.)

ABOVE: The Ace of Aces of World War II was Erich Hartmann, the top ace of Germany and the world with 352 confirmed aerial victories. In his Me-109 he flew 1,425 missions, was in 800 dogfights and his greatest single mission was on August 24, 1944 when he shot down 6 Soviet fighters. On this very same day on his next mission he increased his victories to 11 and became the first man to score 300 kills in air-to-air combat. He shot down 5 American P-51's over Romania in two missions in one day. Hartmann was shot down sixteen times. On September 20, 1943, he was shot down — belly landing behind the Russian lines. After four hours as a virtual Russian prisoner, he escaped back to German lines. Known to the Russians as the "Black Devil of the Ukraine", he spent ten and a half years in Russian prisons after the war. The Russians wanted him to join the East German Air Force or spy for them. Hartmann refused; finally in 1955 he was freed to return to his wife in Germany. He had previously flown the Messerschmitt-262 jet. Eventually he learned to fly jets again, as a Lieutenant Colonel in this new German Air Force, training at Luke AFB in Arizona; becoming a valued attribute in the defense of the West. (National Air and Space Museum.)

The painful warrior famoused for fight,
After a thousand victories, once foil'd,
Is from the books of honor razed quite,
And all the rest forgot for which he toil'd.

WILLIAM SHAKESPEARE (1564 - 1616)
"Sonnet"

THEN & NOW:

Above: Baron von Richthofen's Red Fokker Tri-plane, hence the "Red Baron." The plane had a unique way of making a quick flat turn without banking, reversing direction in four seconds. It had a spectacular climb rate to a 20,000 foot ceiling. Absence of bracing wires and sturdy construction made it difficult to bring down. Richthofen said, "it climbed like a monkey and maneuvered like the devil." (National Air and Space Museum.) Below, Lockheed F104G Starfighter modified by Messerschmitt-Bolkow-Blohm, flies at Mach 2.2; 1,450 miles an hour. Germany's Ernst Heinkel pioneered the jet aircraft in September 1939. And Messerschmitt built the prototype which flew rings around the conventional aircraft. The first production aircraft was delivered in March, 1944; 1320 were delivered to the Luftwaffe. They were used in the last part of the war and it was clear that the jet aircraft was the aircraft of the future. (Photo courtesy German Air Force.)

52

THEN & NOW:

OPPOSITE PAGE TOP: Berlin at Brandenburger Gate in 1911. (Courtesy of the Berlin Archives.) OPPOSITE PAGE BOTTOM: Today the Berlin Wall, that clarion cry of Soviet tyranny, runs barbarically across the picture. 73 refugees have been killed trying to cross to freedom. Is that barbaric? ABOVE: Berlin — promenading on the Unter den Linden in 1911. Note the statue of Frederick the Great in front of the building in the background. (Courtesy of the Berlin Archives.) BELOW: Today the building behind the statue is the East Berlin State Library.

THEN & NOW: ABOVE: Berlin in 1899. The Brandenburger Gate is on the right and the Reichstag looms in the background. (Courtesy of the Berlin Archives.) BELOW: Today, the Berlin Wall runs between the two. OPPOSITE PAGE TOP: Berlin in 1906 at the Hallesches Elevated Train Station. (Courtesy of the Berlin Archives.) OPPOSITE PAGE BOTTOM: Today at that same station in West Berlin.

THEN & NOW: ABOVE: Berlin — Weekend traffic at the Heerstrasse in 1910. (Courtesy of the Berlin Archives.)
BELOW: That same location today, in West Berlin. OPPOSITE PAGE TOP: Berlin in 1913
at the Spittelmarket (Courtesy of the Berlin Archives.) OPPOSITE PAGE BOTTOM: High-
rises have replaced this entire area in East Berlin; vast areas of which were reduced to rubble
in World War II.

56

58

THEN & NOW:

ABOVE LEFT: The Kaiserhof Hotel in Berlin in 1945. Heinrich Hoffman, Hitler's personal photographer wrote, "I myself had a flat on the fourth floor of the Kaiserhof Hotel . . . Hitler moved in and occupied the whole second floor . . . Hitler was very fond of the Kaiserhof." ("Hitler Was My Friend," by Heinrich Hoffman.) Photo courtesy of the National Air and Space Museum. BELOW: Looking into East Berlin across the infamous Berlin Wall. The Kaiserhof Hotel no longer exists; it was located to the right of the picture. Hitler; Eva Braun; Goebbels; his wife and their six youngest children were all either killed or committed suicide in Hitler's Bunker; that bunker is buried beneath the mound of dirt on the left hand side of the picture, against the far wall. OPPOSITE PAGE TOP: View of the Weidendamm Bridge in Berlin in 1898; with the Cafe Mozart in the background. (Courtesy of the Berlin Archives.) OPPOSITE PAGE BOTTOM: That same location today in East Berlin.

59

60

THEN & NOW:

ABOVE: Berlin, Germany in July, 1945 at Potsdamer Station. (Courtesy of the National Air and Space Museum.) Berlin suffered a succession of 1,000-bomber raids. From August 25, 1940 until April 20, 1945 more than 76,000 tons of explosives and incendiary bombs were dropped on Berlin. Berlin's population was 4,332,242 on May 17, 1939 and on October 29, 1946 it was 3,180,383. BELOW: Potsdamer Station was previously located here between the two walls. OPPOSITE PAGE TOP: Cologne, Germany in 1945. Cologne suffered 262 air raids during World War II. 91 of 150 churches were destroyed. The population sank from 768,352 in 1939 to 69,000 in April, 1945. (Courtesy of the National Air and Space Museum.) OPPOSITE PAGE BOTTOM: Today Cologne is a modern, cosmopolitan city. (Photo courtesy of Cologne Tourist Bureau.)

Switzerland

An Alpine Wonderland

64

THEN & NOW:

ABOVE: The Matterhorn in Switzerland that looks the same then and now. In this writer's opinion, the most beautiful place in the world is the Zermatt, Matterhorn region of Switzerland. This view, as seen from the Riffelhorn, painted by the author below. BELOW LEFT: Swiss guide, Joseph, holds the rope while he and the author pose on top of the Riffelhorn, after vertical rock climbing the sheer face of the Riffelhorn above Gornergrot Glacier in 1954; part of the Matterhorn can be seen in the background. BOTTOM RIGHT: The following day, taken from the Matterhorn, looking back at the Riffelhorn.

THEN & NOW:

ABOVE: The Matterhorn as seen from Zermatt, Switzerland. It was first climbed by Edward Whymper, an Englishman, in 1865 (four of his party fell to their death on the descent). The peak of the 14,690 ft. Matterhorn sits exactly on the Italian-Swiss border and the Italian s call it Monte Cervino. Today in good weather, sixty people a day reach the top; a nine-hour round trip. BELOW LEFT: A photo taken during that 1954 climb. BELOW RIGHT: Three decades later, the author now skis the slopes of the Matterhorn — with the Italian Alps in the background (with the same hat).

Venice

The Most Beautiful City in the World

THEN & NOW: ABOVE: Venice, Italy "Capriccio; Rialto Bridge and the Church of San Giorgio Maggiore" in 1750. Oil canvas by Canaletto 1697 - 1768 (Courtesy of the North Carolina Museum of Art.) Capriccio is the Italian word for a joke — it literally means a humorous incident. What Canaletto did in the above painting is take the Church of San Giorgio Maggiore from the Venice Lagoon, on the other side of Venice and put it adjacent to the Rialto Bridge. OPPOSITE PAGE TOP: The Rialto Bridge today. OPPOSITE PAGE BOTTOM LEFT: The Church of San Giorgio Maggiore. OPPOSITE PAGE BOTTOM RIGHT: A side view of the Rialto Bridge with the onion domed tower and cross that is featured in Canaletto's painting.

THEN & NOW: ABOVE: "The Square of Saint Mark's" in 1735 by Canaletto 1697 - 1768. (Courtesy of the National Gallery of Art in Washington D.C. Gift of Mrs. Barbara Hutton.) Four huge bronze horses stand above the main entrance to Saint Mark's Cathedral. They were cast during the time of Alexander the Great. During the Fourth Crusade they were taken from Constantinople (1204). Over 200 years before Columbus discovered America, the horses were placed on the pedestal at Saint Mark's Basilica, where they proudly stand today. BELOW LEFT: The same scene today. BELOW RIGHT: Those four magnificent bronze horses. OPPOSITE PAGE TOP: "Venice, the Quay of the Piazzetta" (early 1730's) by Canaletto. (Courtesy of the National Gallery of Art in Washington D.C. Gift of Mrs. Barbara Hutton.) OPPOSITE PAGE BOTTOM: Today — Venice boasts some 150 canals and more than 400 bridges that are intricate works of art and no automobiles. It is a city of a hundred islands.

THEN & NOW: ABOVE: Venice at the Lagoon; "Bacino de San Marco", by Vanvitelli. (Courtesy of the Los Angeles Library.) BELOW: The same scene today. OPPOSITE PAGE TOP: "View of the Riva degli Schiavoni", by Canaletto 1697 - 1768. (Courtesy of the Toledo Museum of Art; a gift of Edward Drummond Libbey.) In this view from the Lagoon, a portion of the famous Bridge of Sighs can be seen. The bridge got its name because prisoners passed over it from the Palace of the Doges on the left to the prison on the right. OPPOSITE PAGE BOTTOM LEFT: A full view of the Bridge of Sighs as seen from the Lagoon. OPPOSITE PAGE BOTTOM RIGHT: The other side of the Bridge of Sighs — the artist and photographer's dream.

70

72

THEN & NOW:

ABOVE: "Visit of the Doge to the Church of the Salute," an engraving by Brustoloni of a painting by Canaletto published in 1766. (Courtesy of the Los Angeles Library.) For centuries, Venice ruled the seas — a bridge between the East and the West with a navy of 3,300 ships. Marco Polo (1254 - 1324) was Venice's most famous traveler. He was 17 years old when he started his journey in 1271, through Constantinople, Persia, Tibet, the Gobi Desert and on to Khanbaliq (Peking - Beijing). In 1275 he was presented to the Great Kublai Khan of China at Shang-tu. Marco methodically recorded the variety of crops and other products for his merchant family in Venice. In 1295 he arrived back in Venice after 24 years of fabulous adventures. His book, "The Book of Marco Polo" was a smashing success for years to come. It was a geographic and scientific journal and at the same time an adventure story with the intrigue of Oriental Princesses, Kings and Queens. Columbus carried Marco Polo's maps for reference. BELOW: The Church of the Salute today. OPPOSITE PAGE TOP: Venice, Italy, oil on canvas by Canaletto (1697 - 1768) of "View of Piazza San Marco, Facing the Bascilica" in 1740. (Courtesy of the Fogg Art Museum, Harvard University, Cambridge, Mass. Bequest of Grenville L. Winthrop.) Merchant-adventurers stole Saint Mark's body from Alexandria and brought it to Venice and Saint Mark's Cathedral was built as his tomb. The Piazza San Marco is the hub, the very heart-beat of Venice. Today, lovely classical and popular tunes, from two outdoor orchestras waft in the Mediterranean breeze at the elegant outdoor cafes. OPPOSITE PAGE BOTTOM: Saint Mark's Square today.

THEN & NOW: ABOVE: "Capriccio: Piazza San Marco looking South and West" in 1763 by Canaletto 1697 - 1768. (Courtesy of the Los Angeles County Museum of Art — Gift of the Ahmanson Foundation.) The apparent reason that Canaletto called this painting a "Capriccio" was because of the extreme wide angle that it covers. Using a wide angle lens for two different shots only captured a small part of this scene. BELOW LEFT: The 320 foot Bell Tower that overlooks all Venice. In 1595 Fausto Venanico made a parachute drop from this tower. BELOW RIGHT: The Mechanical Bell Strikers that strike the bell atop the tower on the hour. OPPOSITE PAGE TOP: "The Quay with the Library and San Teodoro Column towards the West"; engraving by Brustolini of a Canaletto painting, published in 1766. (Courtesy of the Los Angeles Public Library.) OPPOSITE PAGE BOTTOM: Today.

74

THEN & NOW: ABOVE: "The Entrance to the Grand Canal with the Customs House and the Church of the Salute" in 1735. Engraving by Brustolini (1726 - 1796) of Canaletto's painting. BELOW: The same scene today. OPPOSITE PAGE TOP: "The Bucintora Returning to the Quay on Ascension Day" in 1735. Engraving by Brustoloni of a Canaletto. (Both engravings courtesy of the Los Angeles Public Library.) To escape the barbarian hordes in 523, the Venetians settled on the mud islands. Using small boats they searched for trade and the Republic of Venice grew and grew as the riches of the Orient poured in. Merchant-Princes built palaces that became the most beautiful city in the world. OPPOSITE PAGE BOTTOM: The same scene today.

THEN & NOW: Above, "View of Venice" in 1740 by Canaletto. (Courtesy of the National Gallery of Art from the Widener Collection.) Below, today.

Florence

The Splendor of Michelangelo and the Renaissance

THEN & NOW: Above, Florence Italy and the Arno River. The second bridge is the Ponte Vecchio. In the center the tower to the Vecchio Palace looms and to the right the dome of the Cathedral. Engraving after a drawing by Guiseppe Zocchi published in 1754. (Courtesy of UCLA.) Below, today.

80

THEN & NOW: OPPOSITE PAGE TOP: Florence, Italy the Piazza della Signoria and the festival of San Giovanni. The Vecchio Palace on the left was founded in 1299. The tower was built in 1308. The Fountain of Neptune (1575) and the equestrian monument to the Grand Duke Medici (1594) the benevolent dictator are also shown. Engraving after a drawing by Guiseppe Zocchi published in 1754. OPPOSITE PAGE BOTTOM: That same square today. Notice the exact replica of Michelangelo's famous "David" at the entrance to the Vecchio Palace. ABOVE: Grand Duke Medici, a favorite gathering place for the youth of Florence. The Medici's were a great Italian family who for three centuries were the great catalyst of the Renaissance — they sparked the flame for a Golden Age. (Dwg. courtesy of UCLA.)

82

THEN & NOW:

ABOVE: Looking from the Arno River near the Vecchio Bridge toward the Piazza del Signoria which is dominated by the Tower to the Vecchio Palace on the right. Engraving after a drawing by Giuseppe Zocchi published in 1754. (Courtesy of UCLA.) BELOW: The only thing different today are the clothes worn by the people. OPPOSITE PAGE TOP: The Piazza San Firenze. On the right is the Palazzo del Podesto which was begun in 1250. Notice the cruel and unusual punishment being carried out at the corner of the Palace. Engraving from a drawing by Zocchi published in 1754. (Courtesy of UCLA.) OPPOSITE PAGE BOTTOM: The Palace Tower is being refurbished and a bus has replaced the horse and carriage.

THEN & NOW: ABOVE: Florence, Italy and the Arno River. The bridge in the foreground is the Ponte Santa Trinita (1570) designed by Michelangelo. The bridge was blown up by German mines in 1944, but rebuilt in identical form. In the background is the famous Ponte Vecchio, the oldest bridge in Florence. Often destroyed by floods, the present bridge was finished in 1345. For seven hundred years the Ponte Vecchio has had shops and arcades. It was the only bridge in Florence spared by the Germans. Engraving after a drawing by Guiseppe Zocchi published in 1754. (Courtesy of UCLA.) BELOW: The Ponte Santa Trinita today. OPPOSITE PAGE TOP: The Piazza Santa Trinita with the bridge in the background. The column (1560) was given to Grand Duke Cosimo Medici by Pope Piou IV. Engraving from a drawing by Zocchi published in 1754. (Courtesy of UCLA.) Zocchi was a great artist for including the human drama; notice the scuffle in the center of the picture, oblivious to the ladies on the right. OPPOSITE PAGE BOTTOM: The exact same location today. The youth in the white shirt is looking back over his shoulder at the area of the fight above. Perhaps he wants to go a few rounds.

84

THEN & NOW:

ABOVE: Florence, Italy, the Cathedral on the left was built in 1417, the dome was finished in 1436. To the right, the circular Baptistery was completed in 1150. Dante (1265 - 1321), Italy's greatest poet was baptized there. The tower of the Vecchio Palace can be seen on the skyline on the right. Engraving after a drawing by Guiseppe Zocchi published in 1754. (Courtesy of UCLA.) BELOW: The Cathedral today. OPPOSITE PAGE TOP: The Arno River and the Ponte alla Carrais (bridge) which was first built in 1220 and has been destroyed many times by floods. The German Army last destroyed it, but it was rebuilt in its original form. Engraving after a drawing by Zocchi published in 1754. (Courtesty of UCLA.) OPPOSITE PAGE BOTTOM: The same scene today.

Rome

All Roads Lead to Rome

THEN & NOW: ABOVE: Nero's (A.D. 37 - 68) Circus in Rome. (Photo from a huge replica of ancient Rome at the Museo Della Civilto Romana) BELOW: At the same location as Nero's Circus is Saint Peter's — the largest church in the world; completed in 1626.

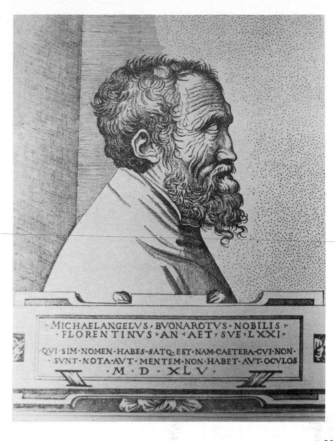

89

THEN & NOW:

ABOVE LEFT: Michelangelo's design for Saint Peter's in Rome. ABOVE RIGHT: Michelangelo himself (1475 - 1564) with the profile of an ex-boxer; from an engraving by Bonasone. (Dwgs. courtesy of the Los Angeles Public Library.) BELOW: Saint Peter's as seen from the Tiber River.

THEN & NOW:

ABOVE: The chariot races from the MGM release "Ben Hur" (1959) Loew's Incorporated, which was filmed in Rome. This scene is comparable to chariot races at Nero's Circus in Rome in the 1st Century. Saint Peter was crucified up-side-down at Nero's Circus. In the 4th Century, Constantine the Great — the first Christian Emperor built a church at the location of Nero's Circus. At this church many Popes and Emperors were crowned — including Charlemagne. OPPOSITE PAGE BOTTOM: At the same location as Nero's Circus is today Saint Peter's. Saint Peter's bones are enshrined directly under the massive dome that was designed by Michelangelo. BOTTOM LEFT: Emperor Caligula had brought an obelisk from Egypt that stood in the center of Nero's Circus. In memory of the thousands of Christians that were killed in Nero's Arena, that same obelisk now stands in the center of the Vatican Piazza.

THEN & NOW:

ABOVE: The Circus Maximus in Rome in the 1st Century; it measured 2,000 by 600 feet and held 180,000 people for chariot races. They also had spectacles with lions, tigers, elephants and gladiators. (Courtesy of the Rome Museum.) BOTTOM LEFT: The Circus Maximus today; with the Imperial Palace on the Palatine, on the far left (see above also.) BOTTOM RIGHT: The Temple of Vesta in the Roman Forum (see opposite page.) OPPOSITE PAGE TOP: Reconstruction of the Roman Forum. OPPOSITE PAGE BOTTOM: That same scene today. The three columns together above the people are from the Temple of Dioscuri above right. (Dwg. of the Forum courtesy of the National Archives.)

94

THEN & NOW:

ABOVE: The top of three columns from the "Temple of Jupiter Tonans" from "Views of Rome" published in 1778 by Piranesi (1720 - 1778) a great artist with pen and brush. (Courtesy of the Library of Congress.) BELOW: Those three columns in the Roman Forum today. Notice how the designs at the top match-up in both pictures. OPPOSITE PAGE TOP: The magnificent "Temple of Venus" and the "Arch of Titus" in the Roman Forum. The Top of the Colosseum can be seen on the right. (Courtesy of the Rome Museum.) OPPOSITE PAGE BOTTOM: A row of columns from the "Temple of Venus" can be seen in front of the Colosseum. The Arch of Titus is in the foreground.

THEN & NOW:

TOP OF PAGE: Rome, Italy at "The Bridge and Mausoleum built by Emperor Hadrian," by Piranesi (1720 - 1778) published in 1778 in "Views of Rome." The tomb was built in 138 A.D. With the passing of a serious plague (589 - 590 A.D.) and Gregory the Great's vision of an angel over the tomb, it became known as Castel Sant Angelo. In 1753 a bronze angel by Pietro Von Werschaffelt was placed atop the fort, the Archangel Michael. (Courtesy of the Library of Congress.) LEFT CENTER: The Castle of St. Angelo and the Tiber River today.

THEN & NOW:

TOP OF PAGE: Rome, Italy. "The Interior of the Pantheon" in 1740 by Giovanni Paolo Panini (1691 - 1765). (Courtesy of the National Gallery of Art, Washington D.C. from the Samual H. Kress Collection.) The Roman Pantheon was begun by Agrippa in 27 B.C. as a building to worship all the gods. It was rebuilt by Hadrian in 120 A.D. in its present form. In 609 A.D. the Pantheon was dedicated as the Church of Saint Maria; Rotunda and for 2,000 years it has served as a temple of worship. Its 142 foot dome is an engineering marvel that has withstood the ages. OPPOSITE PAGE BOTTOM: The Pantheon interior today. BOTTOM RIGHT: The piazza at the Pantheon today.

98

THEN & NOW:

ABOVE: Gladiator (Buddy Baer) defends a maiden (Deborah Kerr) who is tied to the stake. From the MGM release "Quo Vadis" 1951, Loew's Incorporated (Renewed 1979 Metro-Goldwyn Mayer Inc.) BELOW: Joe Louis 1914 - 1981 (Courtesy of the National Archives.) The greatest heavyweight boxer of the 20th Century. He was champion for 12 years. (1937 to 1949) when he retired as an undefeated champion. He defended his title 25 times, scoring 21 knockouts. As a soldier in World War II he fought 96 boxing exhibitions before two million service men all over the world. Known as the "Brown Bomber", he was a devastating counterpuncher who could knock a man out with one punch, from either hand. He was a soft spoken, gracious sportsman, a great patriot and loved by everyone. Ironically, Buddy Baer (the Gladiator above) fought Joe Louis twice — the first time he knocked Louis out of the ring in the first round. Louis climbed back in and won the fight in 7 rounds. Because of a controversial ending to their fight, they fought again and Louis stopped Baer in the first round. In ancient Greek history, no sport was older or more popular than pugilism. It was included in the Olympics in 688 B.C. and in the 1st Century in Rome's Arena's gladiators would bludgeon one another to the death. OPPOSITE PAGE TOP: The Colosseum in the 1st Century. (Courtesy of the Rome Museum.) OPPOSITE PAGE BOTTOM: The Colosseum today.

THEN & NOW:

ABOVE: A scene from "Barabbas" (1962) courtesy of Columbia Pictures. In the Colosseum in Rome, gladiators dueled to the death, with sword and helmet; net and trident; bow and arrow; spear or chariot among a variety of difficult settings that were constructed with all the artistic talents of the 20th Century motion picture industry. Under the Colosseum floor were a maze of tunnels, trap doors and cages to hold animals and prisoners. Sophisticated elevators were also used to raise scenery and participants to the arena. For the celebration of Rome's 1000th Anniversary in A.D. 248, 230 wild animals and 2,000 gladiators were billed to die in the Colosseum. BELOW: The Colosseum today. OPPOSITE PAGE TOP: A scene from "Barabbas" (1962) courtesy of Columbia Pictures. The Emperor, Ivan Trisault raises the symbol of freedom, which means "Barabbas," Anthony Quinn, is a free man in this scene. Historically, gladiators were sometimes also professional athletes lured by the chances of glory and wealth. With rich sponsors, the gladiators also enjoyed the favors of the women from Rome's high society. OPPOSITE PAGE BOTTOM: The Colosseum in busy Rome today.
The Colosseum was built in AD 80. The 100 days of games dedicating the Colosseum was a blood bath. Prisoners fought lions or comrades to the death. The Arena was often flooded and shiploads of men would fight to the death in naval battles, turning the lake red with blood. On hot days an awning was stretched across the Colosseum to shade the combatants and 50,000 spectators.

THEN & NOW: ABOVE: Rome, Italy at "The Arch of Titus" (East Facade) by Piranesi (1720 - 1778) published in 1778 in "Views of Rome." The Arch was built in 81 A.D. to commemorate Titus' capture of Jerusalem. BELOW: Today. OPPOSITE PAGE TOP: Rome, Italy at "The Fountain of Trevi" by Piranesi (1720 - 1778) published in 1778 in "Views of Rome." The song and movie, "Three Coins in the Fountain" glorified this fountain. It was completed by Bracci in 1762. OPPOSITE PAGE BOTTOM: The Fountain of Trevi today. (Dwgs. courtesy of the Library of Congress.)

103

Greece

The French call it "Deja Vu"; as if you'd been there before.
The Parthenon inspired that sensation like a home coming.

THEN & NOW:

ABOVE: The Acropolis as it looked during the golden age. The "Periclean Age" building program made Athens the most beautiful city of antiquity. The huge bronze statue of Athena seen in the square was shipped to Constantinople in the 6th Century by Emperor Justinian. The Acropolis was plundered by Byzantine emperors and barbarian invaders. Most of the destruction was caused in the siege of 1687 when it was occupied by the Turks. (Courtesy of the Los Angeles Public Library.) BELOW: The Parthenon today. OPPOSITE PAGE: The Acropolis today. (Courtesy of Ekdotike Athenon S.A. — Athens Publisher.)

THEN & NOW:

Above, the Propylaea was begun in 437 B.C. and finished in five years. The steps were 71 feet wide; the gap in the middle of the steps was for horses, wagons and chariots. The columns were 5 feet in diameter and 29 feet high. The roof was covered with marble, decorated with gold. These very steps were trod by Alexander the Great and even today there is physical evidence where his shield had hung in the Parthenon. Socrates, Plato and Aristotle have influenced Western reasoning and civilization to this day. (Courtesy of the Los Angeles Public Library.) Below, the Propylaea today.

THEN & NOW: ABOVE: The Parthenon in Athens, Greece as it looked at the time of Christ. (Courtesy of the Los Angeles Public Library.) The Olympian Pericles (495 - 429 B.C.) developed democracy and launched a great building program, the apex of which was the building of the Parthenon on the Acropolis (447 - 432 B.C.) This temple of the Virgin Athena, the Goddess of Wisdom, was the peak of the Doric order in Greek architecture. This magnificent temple was still in all its grandeur until 1687 (for over 2,000 years) when a gunpowder magazine (which the conquering Turks had inside the temple) blew up in the bombardment of the Acropolis by the Venetian general Morosini, making it the ruins it is today. BELOW: The Parthenon today. The French call it "Deja Vu"; as if you'd been there before. The Parthenon evoked that sensation like a homecoming. Although the Taj Mahal is universally called "The most beautiful building in the world," this writer is of the opinion that the Parthenon was the supreme triumph of mankind in building design and nothing before or after has ever equalled its splendor.

THEN & NOW: Above, the Theatre of Dionysus was opened in 534 B.C. As many as 13,000 people crowded the 67 tiers during the spring festivals to listen to the immortal works of Sophocles, Euripides and others do tragic and comic plays. The marble railing was put up by the Romans when the theatre was converted for gladiatorial spectacles. (Courtesy of the Los Angeles Public Library.) Below, the Theatre today.

Egypt

Egypt's glorious contributions to civilization preceded
both Greece and Rome by a thousand years.

THEN & NOW: Above, Napoleon's engineers examining the Sphinx in 1799 from "Description de l'Egypte."
Sketch by Vivant Denon (Courtesy of the Library of Congress.) Below, the Sphinx today.

THEN & NOW:

TOP LEFT: "The Rosetta Stone" was one of the peaks in the history of history. (Ref. Will Durant's, "Story of Civilization.") Photo courtesy of the British Museum where this great black stone slab now rests. The glory of Egypt's history was unknown through the Middle Ages. Egypt was thought to have been a colony of Rome. Hieroglyphics were meaningless — no one knew how to read them. It was a written language that had been forgotten long ago. The unique feature of this 3 ft., 9 inch x 2 ft., 4½ inch stone was that the inscription was in three languages; like many of today's signs that are sometimes in two languages — which say the same thing. First, Akerblod, a Swedish diplomat in 1802, then Thomas Young, an English physicist in 1814, partly deciphered "The Rosetta Stone." The three languages on the stone were Hieroglyphics; Demotic Egyptian and Greek. Ptolemy and Cleopatra were listed on the stone. After more than twenty years of labor, in 1822 one of Napoleon's Egyptologists, Jean Francois Champollion, finally solved the riddle and deciphered the entire inscription; proved the complete Egyptian alphabet and unlocked the door to a glorious lost civilization. And it has since been discovered that the time from Christ until today is a shorter time span than was the glory that was Egypt. In 3150 B.C. King Zoser employed Imhotep to build his tomb, the Step Pyramid and in 30 B.C. Cleopatra put an asp to her breast and died and there had been 3,000 years of splendid and chaotic history between them. TOP RIGHT: Hieroglyphics. CENTER: Napoleon reviewing the French troops at Rosetta where the stone slab was found (From the 400 engravers of Napoleon's 20 volume, "Description de l'Egypte" — Courtesy of the Library of Congress.) OPPOSITE PAGE TOP: The Sphinx in 1799 from, "Description de l'Egypte." At this time most of the Sphinx was completely covered, a composite creature with a lion's body and a human head; it was built 5,000 years ago by King Chephren (3067 - 3011 B.C.) the son of Pharaoh Cheops. OPPOSITE PAGE BOTTOM: The same view today.

112

THEN & NOW:

ABOVE: The Pyramids of Giza. In the background is the Pyramid of Chephren (3067 - 3011 B.C.) and behind it is the Great Pyramid of Cheops (3098 - 3075 B.C.) as they looked when completed and covered with limestone. In the foreground the Pyramid of Mykerinus (3011 - 2988 B.C.) is shown under construction, from a hypothetical model courtesy of the Museum of Science in Boston, Mass. For 4,000 years the Great Pyramid was a spectacular sight; the polished limestone casing became harder and more polished with time and weather, dazzling tourists and travelers until the middle age, when the Arabs (1356) removed 22 acres of the 100-inch-thick casing for hundreds of mina-reted mosques in Cairo. BELOW: Those three pyramids in the same sequence with the Great Pyramid of Giza on the right. In the foreground, "Jimmy Carter" (Gamal Fekrey El Gabry) kissing "Cha Cha Cha" (the camel) while "Charlie Brown" (the donkey) eats sand. OPPOSITE

PAGE TOP: The Great Pyramid of Pharaoh, Cheops, (3098 - 3075 B.C.) in 1799 from "Description de l'Egypte." (Courtesy of the Library of Congress.) The only one of the Seven Wonders of the World that is still standing. At the time of Christ, the Great Pyramid was already over 3,000 years old. Over the centuries the Arabs removed the white limestone casing that completely covered the Pyramid. The debris was over 50 feet high around the base in 1799. The Great Pyramid, even by today's standards, is a masterpiece of technical skill. 2,300,000 blocks that averaged 2½ tons each. The tomb's internal walls used granite blocks, some of which weighed as much as 16 tons, that were brought 500 miles down the Nile River, then pulled across the desert to Giza. OPPOSITE PAGE BOTTOM LEFT: Buzz Gregory (the author's son) poses in front of the Great Pyramid. OPPOSITE PAGE BOTTOM RIGHT: The author standing at the base of the Great Pyramid where the limestone casing is in place.

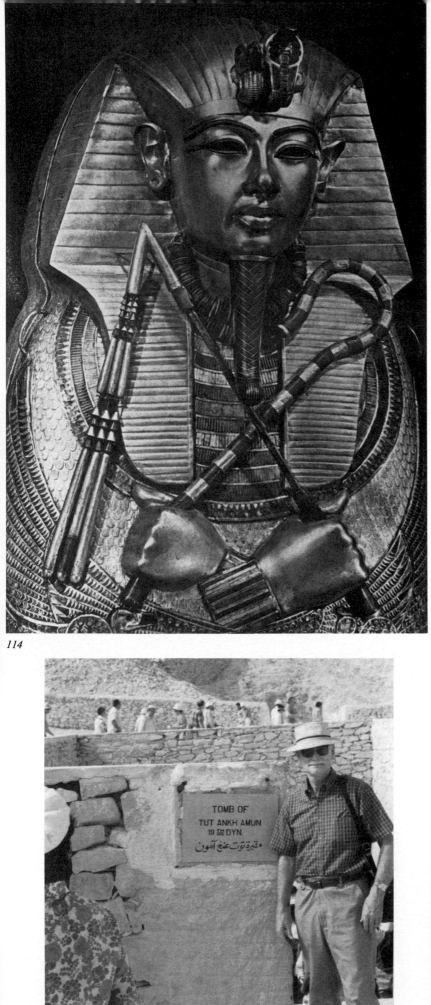

114

THEN & NOW:

ABOVE: The dazzling inner mummy case of gold; now in the Egyptian Museum in Cairo. (Courtesy of the Cairo Museum.) Two hundred years after Tutankhamen was buried. Ramesses VI's tomb was being excavated just above that of Tutankhamen and the workmen threw their waste limestone chips down — completely covering the entrance to the earlier Pharaoh's tomb. Every single pyramid (and there were many) was plundered by ancient grave robbers. Abandoning pyramids the king s excavated the face of the Nile cliffs for tombs. After 1085 B.C. not a single known royal tomb was left intact. The actual discovery of Tutankhamen's tomb in the Valley of the King s in Thebes was on November 4, 1922 when Howard Carter uncovered the steps leading down to the entrance of the connecting rooms of the burial chamber which had been sealed for over 3,000 years. The magnificent treasures were a world wide sensation. Tutankhamen's (1371 - 1352 B.C.) parentage is uncertain; his short rule followed Akhnaton and his wife, the stunningly beautiful Nefertiti. Strong priests dominated Tutankhamen's kingdom; he was nine years old when crowned and nineteen when he died. BELOW LEFT: The author at the entrance to Tut's tomb. BELOW RIGHT: The tomb of Ramesses VI which saved Tut's from the grave robbers is on top, while the stairs down to Tut's are on the bottom.

TOMB OF
TUT ANKH AMUN
18 TH DYN.
مقبرة توت عنخ آمون

THEN & NOW:

Above, the fabulous Queen Nefertiti (courtesy of the Berlin Museum.) Her name literally means, "The Beautiful One is Come." Her bust in the Berlin Museum is proof of her legendary beauty. Tutankhamen (King Tut) the boy Pharaoh's relationship to Nefertiti is bizarre. Her husband was Pharaoh Akhnaton. He clashed with the priests and formed a new god, the sun-god. Because she bore him six daughters, Nefertiti was cast aside and Akhnaton married one of his own daughters. She bore him another daughter. When Akhnaton died at 30, the powerful men behind the throne had a nine year old boy married to Akhnaton's daughter-wife, insuring the boy's claim to the throne. This boy's name was Tutankhamen. Below, graceful feluccas sail the Nile the same as they did 3,350 years ago when Queen Nefertiti travelled the Nile.

116

THEN & NOW:

OPPOSITE PAGE TOP: The Temple of Hathor at Dendera. (Drawn by Denon. From "Description de l'Egypte" — Courtesy of the Library of Congress.) OPPOSITE PAGE BOTTOM: The Temple today after excavation. Notice people enjoyed walking on the roof in both pictures. RIGHT: Reconstruction of the interior of the Temple of Hathor as drawn by David Roberts in 1838, from Roberts, Croly and Brockedon, "The Holy Land." (Courtesy of the Philadelphia Free Library.) ABOVE: The interior of the Temple of Hathor today.

THEN & NOW:

ABOVE: The interior of the Temple of Hathor in all its glory when the Pharaohs reigned supreme. (From "Description de l'Egypte." Courtesy of the Library of Congress.) BELOW: The interior today. OPPOSITE PAGE TOP: A scene from Cecil B. De Mille's, "Ten Commandments." The structure is similar to the royal temple built by Queen Hatshepsut (1522 - 1479 B.C.) in the Valley of the Kings against a cliff 948 feet high. Through palace intrigue, Hatshepsut became the first ruling Queen in history and she controlled Egypt for twenty-two years. (Photo courtesy of Paramount Pictures.) OPPOSITE PAGE BOTTOM: The royal temple of Queen Hatshepsut in the Valley of the Kings today.

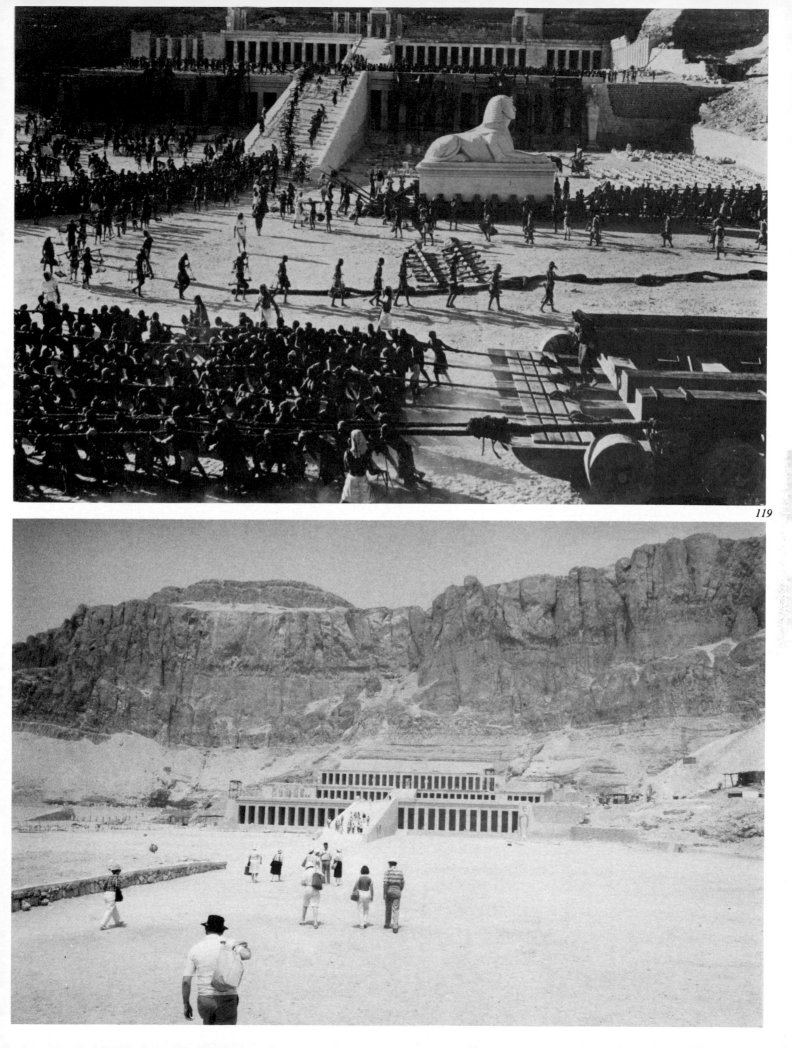

121

THEN & NOW:

OPPOSITE PAGE TOP: Charlton Heston as Moses, an Egyptian Prince, in Cecil B. De Mille's classic, "Ten Commandments." Many historians believe that the Pharaoh of the story of Moses and the Exodus was Ramesses II who reigned from 1304 to 1237 B.C. Will Durant's "Story of Civilization" says Ramesses II was without a doubt one of history's Greatest Rulers and that includes Alexander the Great. He lived for 99 years (1338 - 1237 B.C.); half the monuments of Egypt are from his reign; he was Pharaoh for 67 years; while Egypt dominated Libya; Phoenicia; Syria and Palestine. Ramesses II also fathered 100 sons and 50 daughters. Did he have any other hobbies? You bet he did. He built a canal from the Nile to the Red Sea. And today museums throughout the world boast his statuary taken from Egypt over the centuries. (Photo courtesy of Paramount Pictures.) OPPOSITE PAGE BELOW: The Temple of Luxor today. The walls of the temple glorify Ramesses II military conquests. ABOVE: A scene from Cecil B. De Mille's, "Ten Commandments," erecting an ancient Egyptian obelisk. Queen Hatshepaut had two obelisks 96 feet high and each weighing 325 tons. Special boats were built to transport them from the Aswan quarries down the Nile. Since Greek and Roman times it has been fashionable to ship Egyptian obelisks all over the world: Constantinople; London; Paris; Rome and New York. (Photo courtesy of Paramount Pictures.) BELOW: The obelisk at the entrance to the Luxor Temple.

THEN & NOW:

ABOVE: Egypt, the Temple of Amon-Ra at Karnak. This drawing by Napoleon's troops for the "Description de l'Egypte" shows how it probably looked a thousand years before Christ in the reign of Ramesses II. The Temple of Amon at Karnak took two thousand years to complete and another two thousand years to leave today's classic monuments. Tutankhamen decorated a columned corridor; Ramesses II constructed a pylon; Alexander the Great ordered a new temple built. The huge obelisk honors the female Pharaoh Hatshepsut. (Courtesy of the Library of Congress.) BELOW: The Temple of Karnak today. OPPOSITE PAGE TOP: The interior of the Temple of Karnak today. OPPOSITE PAGE BOTTOM: The entrance at the main pylons is flanked by two rows of rams.

123

THEN & NOW: ABOVE: The Ptolemaic Temple of Edfu as drawn by David Roberts in 1838 from Roberts, Croly and Brockedon, "The Holy Land." (Courtesy of the Free Library of Philadelphia.) Notice how the sand had piled up both in and outside of the temple. BELOW: The Temple of Edfu today. OPPOSITE PAGE TOP: A view from inside the temple looking toward the point from where the exterior drawing was made. This drawing however was made by Dominique Vivant, one of Napoleon's Egyptologists. (Courtesy of the Library of Congress.) OPPOSITE PAGE BOTTOM: The author in the courtyard standing next to a statue of the Falcon God Horus. Notice in the picture above, the shifting desert sands were nearly to the top of the columns. Those are the same columns in the picture below.

124

THEN & NOW:

ABOVE: The Temple of Ombus as drawn by David Roberts in 1838, from Roberts, Croly and Brockedon, "The Holy Land." (Courtesy of the Free Library of the Philadelphia.) BELOW: That same temple today. OPPOSITE PAGE TOP LEFT: The French yachtswoman from an 1894 issue of Harper's Bazaar. (Courtesy of Victorian Fashions and Costumes — Dover Publications.) OPPOSITE PAGE TOP RIGHT:

An Australian yachtswoman, Helen Flaherty, sailing a felluca on the Nile. OPPOSITE PAGE BOTTOM RIGHT: The travelling ladies' spring suit from an 1873 issue of Harper's Bazaar. (Courtesy of Victorian Fashions and Costumes — Dover Publications.) OPPOSITE PAGE BOTTOM LEFT: Austrian beauty Adrienne Niedersuss on the Nile cruise ship. (Note: Both of these lovely ladies were exploring the temple below when that picture was taken.)

126

THEN & NOW:

ABOVE: Napoleon's Egyptologists reconnoiter the Sphinx in 1799 from "Description de l'Egypte." (Courtesy of the Library of Congress.) BELOW: The Sphinx today. OPPOSITE PAGE TOP: The colossal statues at the entrance to the Temple of Ramesses II at Abu Simbel in Nubia in 1838, half covered with drifting sand. Drawn by David Roberts from Roberts, Croly and Brockedon, "The Holy Land." Carved out of the cliff 13 centuries before Christ by Ramesses II. With the construction of the Aswan High Dam across the Nile, the 3,200 year old rock temple would be completely under water. An international fund of $40 million dollars and a prodigious engineering feet cut the temple into huge blocks and reassembled the 67 foot-high colossi 200 feet higher, completing this spectacular feat in 1967. After being concealed for almost 3,000 years, an Italian, Belzoni, in 1817 dug away 31 feet of sand to discover the magnificent interior temple of Ramesses II with beautiful paintings and colossal figures. (Courtesy of the Free Library of Phildelphia.) OPPOSITE PAGE BOTTOM: Abu Simbel today, still after 3,000 years is an awe inspiring sight.

The Holy Land

The Year One Started Here.

130

THEN & NOW:

Above, Christ and John the Baptist at the River Jordan by Gustav Dore (1832 - 1883) published in 1866. (Courtesy of the Los Angeles Public Library.) Below, the author's wife, June, at the River Jordan was a highly emotional experience. A tune held sway over our visit to the Jordan: "Show me that stream called the River Jordan, that's the old stream that I long to cross. Ol' man river, that ol' man river . . . " Jerome Kern's (1885 - 1945) music and Oscar Hammerstein II's (1895 - 1960) immortal words, written as a negro spiritual for "Showboat."

THEN & NOW:

Above, Jesus carrying the cross by G.D. Tiepolo (1727 - 1804) published in 1749. There are 14 stations along the Way of the Cross from the 1st: Jesus condemned by Pilate to the 14th: Jesus is laid in the tomb. Above is the 6th: Veronica wipes the face of Jesus. Below, the Via Dolorosa in Jerusalem marks the path upon which Jesus bore the cross. Over the centuries Christian pilgrims have tread Jesus' last walk before the Crucifixion. (Dwg. courtesy of the Los Angeles Public Library.)

STAZIONE VI.
GESÙ ASCIUGATO DA S.ᵗᵃ VERONICA.
Otten per l'atto pio la Donna amante
L'imago impressa di Gesù penante.

THEN & NOW: ABOVE: "Driving the First Nail" is the title of this emotional drawing by artist, James Tissot (1836 - 1902), which was published in 1896 by St. Hubert Guild. It is from, "The Life of Our Savior Jesus Christ", and is by the Courtesy of Robert F. Looney and the Free Library of Philadelphia.

132

THEN & NOW: ABOVE: The Crucifixion: "Christ on Calvary" by Mihaly Von Munkacsy (1844 - 1900). Etching by the International Art Co. in 1887. (Courtesy of the Library of Congress.) Considering that Jesus Christ was born in the year one, as Ernest Renan (1823 - 1892) affirmed, "The whole of history is incomprehensible without Christ." Painted by Munkacsy in 1884, it is owned by John Wanamaker. Each year during the Easter Season this 14 x 23 foot painting and Munkacsy's "Christ before Pilate" are shown in the court of the Wanamaker store in Philadelphia. BELOW: The site of the Crucifixion — The Church of the Holy Sepulchre in Jerusalem today.

OPPOSITE PAGE BOTTOM: The Church of the Holy Sepulchre as drawn by David Roberts in 1838 for "The Holy Land." Because of the early Christian's reverence for the site of Calvary, Roman Emperor Hadrian (76 - 138) deliberately built a temple to Venus at this location. Empress Helena, the mother of Constantine the Great (285 - 337), was a renown archeologist and she determined to uncover the site of the Crucifixion. After her verification, Constantine built the Church of the Holy Sepulchre in 336, which has remained the chief sanctuary of Christendom. It has been destroyed by invaders twice over the centuries and each time it was restored. Historically, this site has been recognized as the site where Christ was crucified. Today the Church of the Holy Sepulchre looks the same as Robert's drawing in 1838, except that the foreground is now crowded with buildings. (Courtesy of the Free Library of Philadelphia.)

THEN & NOW:

Above, Augustus (63 B.C. - A.D. 14), Emperor of the Roman Empire at its peak for half a century. He pursued Antony and Cleopatra to the death and brought the treasury of Egypt to Rome. He provided spectacular games and gave cash to every citizen and he was worshipped as a god. He renewed safety of the seas and stability in government that would give the vast Empire an unparalleled prosperity for two hundred years (Vatican, Rome.) Below, Ephesus in what is now Turkey. Augustus visited here in 21 B.C. Ephesus became under Augustus the first and greatest metropolis of Asia. Previously as a classic Greek city it boasted the famous Temple of Artemis (or Diana) one of the Seven Wonders of the World; Alexander the Great recaptured the city from the Persians; Jesus' mother, Mary, spent the last years of her life and died in Ephesus; in A.D. 57 St Paul's preaching caused riots here (ref. Acts XIX). The Goths destroyed both the temple and the city in A.D. 262 and neither ever recovered its former glory. (The author at the archway of Hadrian's Temple.)

THEN & NOW: ABOVE: A view of Constantinople (Istanbul) from the Asian section toward the European side in the 18th Century. Behind the lighthouse are the two most famous Mosques, the Blue Mosque and Santa Sophia. Drawing by W.H. Bartlett. (Courtesy of the Free Library of Philadelphia.) BELOW LEFT: Behind the author's late wife, June, in the same sequence as above, left to right: the beautiful Blue Mosque and the historic Santa Sophia which was built and dedicated as a Christian Cathedral in 537 by Emperor Justinian (483 - 565). Rome fell to the barbarians in the 5th Century and Constantinople became the Rome of the East during the Dark Ages, spreading Christianity across the entire Mediterranean basin and Middle East. BELOW RIGHT: Santa Sophia which was built over a thousand years before St. Peters in Rome and its colossal interior is an engineering marvel. It was the largest Christian Church in the world until Constantinople fell to the Turks in 1453 and it became a Mosque.

The Taj Mahal

The Most Beautiful Building in the World.

THEN & NOW:

ABOVE: The Taj Mahal at Agra in India from across the Jumna River. Aquatint by Thomas and William Daniell in 1801. (Courtesy of the Library of Congress.) BELOW: Today. OPPOSITE PAGE TOP: The Taj Mahal from the garden. Aquatint by Thomas and William Daniell in 1801. (Courtesy of the Library of Congress.) The Taj Mahal was built in 1643. For centuries, many people have said that the Taj Mahal is the most beautiful building in the world. Its story is a true love story. The Mogul Emperor Shah Jahan built the Taj Mahal as a tomb to his beloved wife called Mumtaz Mahal "chosen one of the palace" (shortened to Taj Mahal.) She died in childbirth in 1631. Architects from Persia, India and all over Asia designed the mausoleum, which took 20,000 workmen twelve years to build. Jewelers cut gems and laid them into the stone scrolls and flowers. Imprisoned by his son who usurped the throne, the Mogul Emperor spent the rest of his life in a tower close by from where he could see the beautiful Taj Mahal. OPPOSITE PAGE BOTTOM: The Taj Mahal today.

Hong Kong
From Chop-Sticks to Transistors

THEN & NOW:

ABOVE LEFT: The contrast between a Chinese Junk and the modern high-rise buildings on the island of Hong Kong. BELOW: Again a Chinese Junk contrasts, this time to an international freighter, with Kowloon and the famous Ferry Pier in the background. OPPOSITE PAGE TOP: A view of Hong Kong from East Point in 1856, during the expedition of an American Squadron to the China Seas and Japan from 1852 to 1856 under M.C. Perry. (Courtesy of the Library of Congress.) OPPOSITE PAGE BOTTOM: That same view today. Hong Kong is a British crown colony of 5.5 million people, 98% of whom are ethnically Chinese, many had fled China's Communism. In 1997 Hong Kong reverts to China who has pledged to keep the present capitalist system and let it remain a free port.

140

THEN & NOW:

ABOVE: The Hong Kong City Hall in 1879, during President Grant's world tour. (Courtesy of the Library of Congress.) BELOW: The Hong Kong City Hall today is the building with the checkered windows on the left. OPPOSITE PAGE TOP: Hong Kong as seen from East Point on May 16, 1879 during President Grant's world tour. (Courtesy of the Library of Congress.) OPPOSITE PAGE BELOW: That same view today.

143

THEN & NOW:

ABOVE: Nancy Kwan jitterbugging in a scene from, "The World of Suzie Wong," (1960) an excellent motion picture that glamourized Hong Kong's ladies of the night. (Courtesy of Paramount Pictures.) BELOW: The location in Hong Kong where the exterior shots were made for the movie. Today it is a Curio Shop instead of a Bar and Hotel as shown in the movie. Now I ask you, would you rather see an exterior shot of that old hotel or the picture shown above? OPPOSITE PAGE TOP: Hong Kong as seen from Kowloon in 1842 from an engraving by T. Allom and Capt. Stoddart R.N. (Courtesy of the Los Angeles Public Library.) OPPOSITE PAGE BOTTOM: The Hong Kong skyline as seen at night from Kowloon. ("The World of Suzie Wong" photo - Copyright © 1960 PARAMOUNT PICTURES CORPORATION ALL RIGHTS RESERVED)

144

THEN & NOW: OPPOSITE PAGE TOP: Fort Victoria in Kowloon in 1841, from an engraving by T. Allom and Lt. White. (Courtesy of the Los Angeles Public Library.) OPPOSITE PAGE BOTTOM: Believe it or not, that same scene today. The location of Fort Victoria was in the old walled city of Kowloon. That old section shown is surrounded by high-rises and due to reclamation and the new Hong Kong Airport it is today miles from the water. ABOVE: The Bay and Island of Hong Kong in 1838, from a lithograph by A. Borget. (Courtesy of the Los Angeles Public Library.) BELOW: That same scene today.

145

Peking (Beijing)

The Great Wall of China, the Largest Man-Made Structure in the World.

THEN & NOW:

ABOVE: A view of Pa Ta Ling Gate in the Great Wall of China in 1899 (courtesy of the Los Angeles Public Library) as seen from the top of the wall. BELOW: The same location today. OPPOSITE PAGE TOP: Another view of the Pa Ta Ling Gate. OPPOSITE PAGE BOTTOM: That same view today. China has refurbished many portions of the Great Wall. Ch' in Shih Huang Ti began building the Wall in the 3rd Century B.C. He was China's first emperor and the word China is from his name. During his reign, large sections of the 2,500 mile long wall were built, i.e. including its peripheral off-shoots. Because the wall kept the barbarians out, the Huns moved west into Europe and down into Italy. Will Durant said, "Rome fell because China built a wall." The Huns plunged Europe into the Dark Ages. Despite the Great Wall, the barbarians eventually broke through and for awhile put an end to the growth of civilization. (19th Century view courtesy of the Los Angeles Public Library.)

148

THEN & NOW:

OPPOSITE PAGE TOP: An 1859 drawing of the Great Wall. (Courtesy of the Los Angeles Public Library.) The artist appears to have romanticized and taken liberties, because the wall seems to go on and on. However, in the photo on the OPPOSITE PAGE BOTTOM: The Great Wall does go on and on. ABOVE RIGHT: An enlarged section of the Great Wall from the top of the photo on the bottom of the opposite page. BELOW: An enlarged section from the upper right hand corner from the same photo.

THEN & NOW: Above, an artist's conception of the Great Wall of China in the 19th Century. Below, the Great Wall today is the major Chinese tourist attraction, especially for the Chinese people. (19th Century picture courtesy of the Los Angeles Public Library.)

150

THEN & NOW: Above, Peking (Beijing) China at the Western Gate in 1841, from an engraving by T. Allom. (Courtesy of the Los Angeles Public Library.) Below, the same view today. The waterway, bridge and wall now belong to the past; replaced by a broad street. (QIANMEN-DONGOAJIE STREET.)

151

152

153

THEN & NOW:

OPPOSITE PAGE TOP: Peking (Beijing) China in 1700, from an engraving by Auriques. (Courtesy of the Los Angeles Public Library.) OPPOSITE PAGE BOTTOM: The Wumen Gate (Meridian Gate) to the Forbidden City. Peking has two walled cities. The Tartar City with walls two and one-quarter miles long surrounded by a moat. The Forbidden City contains the Imperial Palaces which today are museums built in 1406 - 1420 during the Ming Dynasty. ABOVE: Inside the huge Forbidden City, magnificent temples, pavilions, canals and bridges make up the Imperial Palaces. Peking was the starting point for the famous "Silk Road." Caravans of camels crossed mountains, deserts and rivers to reach India and eventually Europe. BELOW: Chinese art at its finest at the Imperial Palace in the Forbidden City.

THEN & NOW: Above, the Imperial Palace Gardens in Peking (Beijing) in 1841, from an engraving by T. Allom. (Courtesy of the Los Angeles Public Library.) Built 800 years ago, they served as royal gardens for the Kin, Yuan, Ming and Qing dynasties. The Tibet-style White Dagoba was built on the top of Jade Isle in 1651 to store Lamaist scriptures and mantles. Below, the same view today.

154

Shanghai

Shanghai conjured adventure; it literally meant the kidnapping of a sailor for the crew of a Clipper Ship.

THEN & NOW: Above, Shanghai, China as seen from across the river in 1874. (Courtesy of the Library of Congress.) Below, Shanghai as seen from across the river today.

THEN & NOW:

Above, Shanghai, China at the Bund, i.e. the waterfront, in the early part of the 20th Century. Noted as the wildest seaport in the world, Shanghai had about 30,000 prostitutes and thousands of opium addicts. Its name literally could mean the kidnapping of a sailor for the crew of a Clipper Ship. Shanghai still conjures romance and adventure, the lure of the Orient and faraway places. But that Shanghai is gone. Photo by world traveller and photographer, Burton Holmes. (Courtesy of the Library of Congress.) Shanghai today has 12 million people; while China itself has 1.1 billion people. OPPOSITE PAGE TOP: The Bund today. OPPOSITE PAGE BOTTOM: Another view of the Bund today. Shanghai is the gateway to the Changjiang (Yangtze) River basin and it is the most important seaport in China.

THEN & NOW: Above, Shanghai, China at English Town. Photo taken during President Grant's world tour on May 27, 1879. (Courtesy of the Library of Congress.) Below, the same location today at the Wusong River (Suzhou Creek.) Notice the string of boats passing under the bridge.

158

Tokyo
The New Industrial Revolution

THEN & NOW:

Above, an early Japanese electric train. (Courtesy of the Diet Library.) Below, the Japanese Bullet Train which makes scheduled runs from Nagoya to Yokohama (196.5 miles) in 105 minutes at 112.3 mph. (Courtesy of the Japanese National Railways.) Fujiyama in the background is the highest mountain in Japan (12,388 ft.), it is a dormant volcano that last erupted in 1707.

THEN & NOW:

Above: Tokyo, Japan on September 1, 1945. The Asukasa section of Tokyo — the most populated "KU" or ward in the world — 80,000 to 140,000 persons to the square mile of this area. Photo by 20th Air Force. (Courtesy of the National Air and Space Museum.) The night of March 9, 1945 (at 10:30 P.M.) to March 10 (2:30 A.M.) when the last of 329 B-29 bombers left Tokyo was the night that Tokyo became a living hell. It surpassed any of the horrific raids on Hiroshima; Nagasaki; Berlin; Dresden or Hamburg. 120,000 died in the war's worst raid. The firebombs (cylindrical canisters) and gusting winds caused "firestorms" that drew the oxygen, causing buildings to literally explode. 13 square miles were devastated; at least 120,000 people were killed and one Japanese government estimate after the war stated that 190,000 were dead or missing. (Ref.: An Associated Press article by Richard Pyle titled, "The night Tokyo became a living hell," in the March 10, 1985 Los Angeles Examiner.) Below, that same view as above today; the street in the foreground running horizontal across the picture is the same street running horizontal in the photo above; the heart of the business and shopping center of Asakusa.

THEN & NOW: Above, Tokyo, Japan on September 1, 1945. The ruins of the Asukasa section of Tokyo. (Photo by 20th Air Force, courtesy of the National Air and Space Museum.) Below, today the Asakusa District is criss crossed with streets that are covered to make shopping arcades.

THEN & NOW: Above, Tokyo, Japan in September, 1945 showing the bomb damage after B29 incendiary attacks (Air Force photo, courtesy of the National Air and Space Museum.) This picture is looking west across the Sumida River towards the small vertical Kenda River. Below, today looking northwest; on the right of the picture at the same location is the Asakusahashi Railroad Bridge; the left bridge has been relocated closer to the Kenda River.

THEN & NOW: Above, Tokyo, Japan on September 1, 1945. Results of the B29 bombing of the Ginza District of Tokyo. (Photo by 20th Air Force, courtesy of the National Air and Space Museum.) Tokyo in 1942 had a population of 6,916,000. By September 1945, little was left standing in the heart of the city and the population had been reduced to 2,777,000. Below, the very heart of the Ginza District today at the corner of Ginza and Harumi Avenues — looking down Ginza. The circular high-rise on the right had a unique Friday event. Five slender Japanese chorus girls would literally stop traffic at this Ginza intersection by putting on snappy synchronized dance routines in the window of the fourth floor; the entire building's wall is clear glass.

163

THEN & NOW: ABOVE: Trolleys, pedestrians and an early vintage car on Ginza Avenue early in the century at the Hattori clock-tower. (Photo courtesy of the Tokyo Metropolitan Records and Archives Institute.) BELOW: At the same location a clock-tower still dominates this famous intersection on the northwest corner of Ginza and Harumi Avenues in the heart of Tokyo. OPPOSITE PAGE TOP: The Nihombashi Bridge which was built in 1911. (Photo courtesy of the Tokyo Metropolitan Records and Archives Institute.) OPPOSITE PAGE BOTTOM: Today the Nihombashi Bridge is covered by an Expressway in downtown Tokyo.

THEN & NOW: ABOVE: A view from the Tokyo Imperial Palace across the Plaza after the September 1, 1923 earthquake; with survivors camping on the Plaza. (Photo courtesy of the Tokyo Metropolitan Records and Archives Institute.) BELOW: The horizon has moved a lot closer to the Imperial Palace, with high-rise hotels and office buildings that now surround the Palace. OPPOSITE PAGE TOP: An early Japanese train and crew pose proudly on the bridge. (Courtesy of the Diet Library.) OPPOSITE PAGE BELOW: The Bullet Train crosses over a bridge in the Ginza District of downtown Tokyo.

166

Hiroshima

The Atomic Age Started Here

THEN & NOW:

ABOVE: On August 6, 1945 at 8:15 in the morning, Hiroshima was the first city to be hit with an atomic bomb. The bomb exploded 1,900 feet in the air over the domed building shown in this picture. Four square miles in the heart of Hiroshima were instantly devastated; the blast and radiation from this one bomb killed 140,000 people. BELOW: Today that same building (A-Bomb Dome) is located in Peace Memorial Park surrounded by a clean, beautiful industrial city. OPPOSITE PAGE TOP: Looking west on Aioi dori Avenue in August 1945 after the bomb was dropped on Hiroshima. OPPOSITE PAGE BOTTOM: The same exact location as above; today looking west on busy Aioi dori Avenue from Chuo dori Avenue. (WWII photos courtesy of the National Air and Space Museum.)

THEN & NOW: ABOVE: Hiroshima in August 1945 — looking west across the Tenma River at complete devastation and rubble. BELOW: Today at the Tenma River bridges on the left side of the above photo, which have been relocated. (Above photo courtesy of the National Air and Space Museum.) OPPOSITE PAGE TOP: The Hondori clock tower on the Hondori shopping street. The position of the tower shows the force of the blast — 700 meters from the center. OPPOSITE PAGE BOTTOM: The Hondori Shopping Street today. (Above photo courtesy of the National Air and Space Museum.)

THEN & NOW: ABOVE: Hiroshima in August 1945. (Courtesy of the National Air and Space Museum.) The dark strip running across the picture under the street is a canal, this is today Chuo dori Avenue, one of the main streets in Hiroshima. BELOW: The street in the left foreground is the same street — where the man is riding the bicycle above; it now continues straight instead of turning and other new streets have been relocated. OPPOSITE PAGE TOP: 1.3 kilometers east of the epicenter at the Inari-cho streetcar bridge. (Courtesy of the Hiroshima Peace Memorial Museum.) OPPOSITE PAGE BELOW: A Coca Cola advertising streetcar crosses over the modern bridge at the same Inari-cho crossing.

172

THEN & NOW: ABOVE: Looking south across the gnarled trees of Shukkeien Park in Hiroshima in August 1945. (Courtesy of the National Air and Space Museum.) BELOW: That same scene today. OPPOSITE PAGE TOP: Hondori, the business section 400 - 500 meters from the center of the blast which was at the bombed out dome that can be seen in the distance. (Courtesy of the Hiroshima Peace Memorial Museum.) OPPOSITE PAGE BELOW: That same section of Hiroshima today.

174

Nagasaki

Up From the Dust

THEN & NOW: ABOVE: Nagasaki, Japan on September 12, 1945; and devastation of the second atomic bomb. (Courtesy of the National Air and Space Museum.) On August 9, 1945, Nagasaki was the second city to be struck by an atomic bomb. Surrender negotiations were initiated by the Japanese the next day. BELOW: The exact same location today; see the railing in both pictures on the right side, for the bridge over a creek. The epicenter of the bomb was in the park with the trees on the right. In the above picture it is located just above the head of the girl with her hands together, and at that spot today stands the column shown on the opposite page. OPPOSITE PAGE: The epicenter of the atomic bomb dropped on Nagasaki. A plaque in the park at this column states: "This is the epicenter of the Atomic Bomb. At 11:02 A.M., August 9, 1945 the Atomic Bomb dropped from the B29; it exploded 1,600 feet in the air above this black stone pillar. It completely destroyed 12,900 houses; killed 73,884 people (many died later) and injured 74,909 people."

177

THEN & NOW: ABOVE: The Shimonokawa Iron Bridge; 250 meters from the center of the bomb blast. The bridge shifted one meter off the girders. (Photo courtesy of the Nagasaki Atomic Bomb Museum.) BELOW: That same bridge today. OPPOSITE PAGE TOP: Atomic bomb damage in Nagasaki on October 15, 1945. Photo from a plane from the U.S.S. Chenago from 300 feet. (Courtesy of the National Air and Space Museum.) OPPOSITE PAGE BOTTOM: The same area today.

Hawaii

Paradise Found

THEN & NOW: OPPOSITE PAGE TOP: "Hula, Hula or Dancing Girls," was the title of this engraving published in 1874 in Charles Nordoff's "Northern California, Oregon and the Sandwich Islands." Capt. James Cook discovered the Islands on January 20, 1778 and he named them after his sponsor, the Earl of Sandwich; who is also famous for naming the sandwich a sandwich; which is another story. OPPOSITE PAGE BELOW: Hula girls at the famous Kodak Hula Show in Honolulu. ABOVE: Diamond Head and Waikiki in 1874. This engraving was also published in 1874 in Nordoff's book. BELOW: This scene symbolizes Hawaii today. The famous Waikiki Beach hotels with their marvelous views of the blue and often emerald Pacific; where you can swim 300 yards out into the ocean and the water will be up to your waist. It is truly paradise. (Dwgs. courtesy of the Los Angeles Public Library.)

THEN & NOW: ABOVE: Honolulu, Hawaii in 1874. Engraving first published in 1874 in Charles Nordoff's, "Northern California, Oregon and the Sandwich Islands." (Courtesy of the Los Angeles Public Library.) BELOW: That same scene today. OPPOSITE PAGE TOP: Waikiki Beach, Honolulu in 1896. (Courtesy of the California Historical Society.) OPPOSITE PAGE BOTTOM: Waikiki Beach today. Riding the catamaran shown in the picture out to sea and around Diamond Head was fun. They hold about 25 people. The return trip was sensational: dolphins escorted us in, leaping high in the air. Now a catamaran running with the wind can really move — the dolphins at the same time were actually swimming rings around the boat. Outrigger canoes and the catamarans make their long run back to shore riding the crest of a wave and tooting their polynesian horns to clear the way. Streaking through the water they float right up on the sand where the riders jump out laughing and chattering.

182

THEN & NOW:

ABOVE: Honolulu Harbor over a hundred years ago, in 1880. Nunanu Valley is to the left and the Punchbowl is in the background. (Courtesy of the National Archives.) BELOW: The same location today. The luxurious cruise ship, Royal Viking Star, a floating pleasure palace, is moored at Hawaii's famous Aloha Tower which can be seen in the center of the picture in front of the striped building. During the Golden Age of motion pictures (the thirties), the Aloha Tower dominated the skyline; it symbolized Hawaii and whenever the screenwriter had a transition to Hawaii, the Aloha Tower and pier was the establishing shot; today it is Diamond Head and the white high-rises along Waikiki Beach. OPPOSITE PAGE TOP: In the most spectacular photograph of December 7, 1941, the destroyer Shaw explodes, after getting hit by a bomb at Pearl Harbor in Hawaii. (Courtesy of the U.S. Navy.) In the attack the Japanese came in simultaneously from several directions and of 400 American military aircraft only 38 planes got off the ground and 10 of these were shot down. The Japanese lost 27 aircraft, one large submarine and 5 midget (2-man) subs. The Japanese attack on Pearl Harbor was a brilliant tactical operation. However, strategically it was a failure; because it awoke the isolationist sleeping giant that is America. OPPOSITE PAGE BOTTOM: Pearl Harbor today. The location of the destroyer, Shaw, was on the right hand side of the picture, where she was located in a floating drydock when she was hit.

THEN & NOW: Above, the explosion of the magazine in the Battleship Arizona as seen from Ford Island, where almost all of the Catalina search and patrol seaplanes and carrier aircraft were destroyed in the first attack. (Courtesy of the U.S. Navy.) Below, looking across Ford Island today, the white memorial to the 1,102 men who are still entombed in the once proud battleship Arizona, can be seen in the distant center of the picture below. The average age of these men was 19 and it is a deeply emotional experience to see their names listed on the inside wall of this shrine. Over 2,400 Americans were lost this day, of which 2,000 were Navy personnel and over half of these were lost on the Arizona.

THEN & NOW:

Above, Battleship Row taken by a Japanese pilot at the start of the attack on Pearl Harbor on December 7, 1941. (Courtesy of the U.S. Navy.) Left to right are the Nevada; Arizona; Tennessee; and the West Virginia (moored outboard of the Tennessee); Maryland and the Oklahoma (moored outboard of the Maryland.) Also at Pearl were the Battleship California; Pennsylvania and Utah. The smoke in the background is rising from Hickam Field. The Oklahoma rolled over and sank with over 400 fatalities. The West Virginia and the Nevada were sunk as well as the California which lost almost 100 of her crew. The Utah capsized after two torpedo hits. When the Arizona sank over a thousand perished. Below, today Battleship Row is the U.S.S. Arizona Memorial which traverses the sunken hull of the gallant Battleship Arizona and the mooring quays can be clearly seen in both pictures.

DIAMOND HEAD, BEACH OF WAIKIKI

THEN & NOW:

ABOVE: Diamond Head and the Beach of Waikiki in 1919. (Courtesy of the Library of Congress.) BELOW: The same scene today from a helicopter. OPPOSITE PAGE TOP: Surfing off Waikiki in 1920. (Courtesy of the Bishop Museum.) "Look Maw, I'm standing up!" Two legends of Hawaiian surfing are Duke Kahanamoku and George Freeth who was brought to Redondo Beach, California to introduce surfing to the United States by Henry E. Huntington. Freeth was the son of a Hawaiian princess and an American father. The Duke was pure Hawaiian stock and he held the world's record for the 50 and 100 meter freestyle swim sprints. He won three gold and two siver medals in the Olympics. Johnny Weissmuller finally beat the Duke in the 100 meter freestyle by 0.25 second for the gold and the Duke settled for the silver. OPPOSITE PAGE BELOW: A photo by Hawaiian surf photographer, Vince Cavataio, renown as the best surf photographer in the world. This is Hawaii's famous "Banzai Pipeline."

San Francisco

From the Barbary Coast to the Towering Golden Gate Bridge

THEN & NOW: ABOVE: San Francisco's famous Trans America Pyramid Building framed by the rigging of 3 masted schooner "C.A. Thayer." Built in 1895, she was the last commercial sailing vessel flying the American Flag. THEN & NOW all in one picture. OPPOSITE PAGE TOP: San Francisco in 1851. "View from Signal Hill." Lithograph by Boosey after a sketch by Capt. Collinson. Printed by M & N Hanhart. Published by Ackerman & Co. in 1851. (Courtesy of the Library of Congress.) BELOW: A montage of pictures from the top of Coit Tower which presently sits on that same hill. Most of the wharfs and adjacent water in the center of the 1851 lithograph were filled in over the years, extending the coastline out into the bay. The Oakland Bay Bridge crosses to Yerba Buena Island, seen in both pictures.

Birdseye View of San Francisco From Top of Wrecked City Hall Dome.

(Picture of the Dome Is Shown in Upper Right-Hand Corner.)

Supplement to San Francisco Examiner, June 10, 1906.

THEN & NOW:

ABOVE: "Birdseye View of San Francisco From the Top of the Wrecked City Hall Dome" as it appeared in the San Francisco Examiner of June 10, 1906 — the aftermath of the earthquake and devastating fire of April 18, 1906. (Courtesy of the Library of Congress.) BELOW: The same scene today, from a high rise located to the right of the City Hall above. A reference point in both photos is Yerba Buena Island in the above photos; the tip of that same island can be seen below as part of the Oakland Bay Bridge. The elegant new City Hall and Dome can be seen below. Also, the street running diagonal across the right hand side of the above photo is Market Street. This same street can be seen on the extreme right hand side (opposite page) below. OPPOSITE PAGE TOP: San Francisco's famous Steiner Street Victorian Houses at Alamo Park captures the style of old San Francisco. In the background, the Trans America Building and other high-rises have become the modern symbol of the city noted for its cable cars and bridges. Then and Now — all in one picture.

192

193

THEN & NOW:

ABOVE: On opening day, May 27, 1937, pedestrians enjoy walking down the middle of the "Golden Gate Bridge" in San Francisco; while a squadron of well-grouped biplanes soar between the stanchions. (Courtesy of the San Francisco Chronicle.) For 27 years the "Golden Gate Bridge" was the Longest Suspension Bridge in the World at 4,200 feet. In 1964 the "Verrazano Narrows Bridge" in New York City reached 4,260 feet. OPPOSITE PAGE TOP: Four hundred years after Sir Francis Drake's initial voyage, (he circumnavigated the world between 1577 and 1580), this replica of "The Golden Hind" is greeted by a flotilla as it sails under the bridge. This classic photograph was taken by Robert Cameron and is in color in his spectacular book, "Above San Francisco"; new collection of nostalgic and contemporary aerial photographs. (Cameron and Company, 235 Montgomery Street, San Francisco, CA 94104 — $19.95.) OPPOSITE PAGE BOTTOM: The "Royal Viking Star" passes the towering Golden Gate Bridge. (Courtesy of the Royal Viking Line.) All three photographs project the sentiment of celebration.

THEN & NOW:

ABOVE: San Francisco on December 26, 1911. (Courtesy of the Library of Congress.)
BELOW: That same skyline as it appears today. The gray building on the right side of the above photo with the overhanging cornice and seven rounded window tops has been replaced with the present Holiday Inn below which is the building with the tapered base sitting near the Trans America Pyramid Building. In the background is the Oakland Bay Bridge and Yerba Buena Island which has the largest diameter road tunnel in the world — 76 ft. wide, 58 ft. high and 540 ft. long. On its two decks, more than 35,000,000 vehicles pass every year. OPPOSITE PAGE TOP LEFT: The author's late wife, June, during World War II as a U.S. Navy WAVE in San Francisco's Chinatown — notice the pagoda, church clock and now classic cars. And right, over 40 years later, posing in the exact same spot — notice the high-rise behind the church. OPPOSITE PAGE BOTTOM RIGHT: The author, Howard Gregory, poses in front of a DC3 during World War II (82nd A/B). And left, over 40 years later, posing in front of a DC3 today. The rocking-chair is the insignia for Parachutists Over Phorty Society (POPS) i.e. those who parachute jump after age 40.

THEN & NOW: ABOVE: San Francisco after the violent earthquake of April 18, 1906; followed by an inferno that swept through the city; most of the central business and residential districts were demolished. This view is from Chinatown looking toward Nob Hill; the tall gutted building is the Fairmont Hotel. By 1915 much of the city was rebuilt for the Panama-Pacific International Exposition. (Courtesy of the Library of Congress.) BELOW: The same view from Chinatown today; the tall building in the center of the picture is the new Fairmont Hotel Tower; the old Fairmont Hotel can be seen just behind and to the left of the Tower.

198

Los Angeles

Hooray for Hollywood!

THEN & NOW:

ABOVE: The Babylonian Sequence from "Intolerance" filmed in Hollywood near the intersection of Hollywood and Sunset Boulevards in 1916 by D.W. Griffith, the motion picture pioneer and genius. Many superlatives have been designated about Hollywood productions, but the Babylonian set was truly the most spectacular set ever constructed for a motion picture. The towers were 135 feet high and for years they were a famous landmark that could be seen from all over the Los Angeles basin. Griffith mounted the camera platform on a tower with an elevator to move vertically and at the same time the tower was on tracks that could move the picture horizontal to close in on the dancing girls and some 4,000 extras. Babylon, including the hanging Gardens of Babylon, one of the Seven Wonders of the World have long ago passed into antiquity, vanishing without a trace. BELOW: The exact location where the above spectacular scene was shot. (Babylonia photo courtesy of the Library of Congress.)

THEN & NOW:

ABOVE: Hollywood in 1905. The street running horizontally across the center of the picture is Hollywood Boulevard. The building with the two towers to the extreme left of Hollywood Boulevard is the grand old Hollywood Hotel. The house with the oriental cupola in the foreground became the home of silent screen star Conway Tearle. (Courtesy of the California Historical Society.) BELOW: Today the cupola is between the two palm trees in the center of the picture. That building is presently the home of the American Society of Cinematographers. The striped building in the upper left is the Paramount Theatre; part of the Chinese Theatre (the home of the famous foot-prints in cement) can be seen to the left of the high-rise in the foreground.

OPPOSITE PAGE TOP: Looking north toward Hollywood Hills at the intersection of Wilshire and Fairfax in 1920. Mercury Aviation Company can be seen on the hanger on the left. The company was formed by Cecil B. De Mille and was the first official commercial airline in California's history with fields in San Diego, Long Beach, Pasadena, Bakersfield, Fresno and San Francisco. De Mille was himself an Air Corps pilot. Lt. Jimmy Doolittle performed stunts at an Air Show at the field and Capt. Eddie Rickenbacker flew in the first metal cabin plane to be used in the United States, which De Mille bought from the Junkers Aircraft Corporation. (Courtesy of the California Historical Society.) OPPOSITE PAGE BELOW: The exact same location today.

THEN & NOW:

ABOVE: Universal Studios, when the San Fernando Valley was a prairie, in the early part of the century. The diagonal road in the distant left became Ventura Boulevard. (Photo courtesy of Eddie Brandt.) BELOW: The same scene today at Universal City. The Ventura Freeway now runs diagonally across the bustling Valley. In the early years, Universal made classics, e.g., "The Phantom of the Opera" (1925) and "All Quiet on the Western Front" which won the Oscar for the Best Picture of the Year 1930. Boris Karloff's "Frankenstein" series began in 1931. Classic pictures of the modern era include, "The Sting"; "The Great Waldo Pepper" and "The Eiger Sanction" which were released through Universal.

OPPOSITE PAGE TOP: An aerial view of 20th Century Fox Studios in 1940. The main studio offices are in the lower left. Above them is the back lot where most of the sets stood. To the right is one of the western towns, e.g. "My Darling Clementine," was shot here. And close to the western town is the lake where water scenes were photographed. Darryl F. Zanuck (1902 - 1979), a giant in the film industry was one of the founders of 20th Century in 1933. He was previously a scriptwriter for the "Rin Tin Tin" series and as an executive producer he helped develop the careers of Edward G. Robinson, James Cagney, Tyrone Power, Gregory Peck and numerous other super stars. Zanuck as Chairman of the Board of 20th produced many of the classic films that will remain for generations; John Ford's memorable motion pictures will stand the test of time. (Courtesy of the Bison Archives.) OPPOSITE PAGE BOTTOM: Century City today; the high-rises on the distant left are luxury condominiums on Wilshire Blvd.

THEN & NOW:

ABOVE: The Los Angeles City Hall in 1928 when it was completed. At 28 stories it was the tallest building in the city and the only structure in town allowed to rise over 150 feet (because of earthquakes and fires.) Courtesy of the California Historical Society. BELOW: Looking north at the new L.A. with the Harbor Freeway on the left and City Hall on the right. New building techniques and safety measures have transformed the Los Angeles skyline.

OPPOSITE PAGE TOP LEFT: The "Paris Calling Costume" from the October 30, 1897 cover of "Harper's Bazaar" America's glamorous illustrated women's magazine of the gay nineties. OPPOSITE PAGE TOP RIGHT: Los Angeles model, Dawn Morris, today. OPPOSITE PAGE BOTTOM RIGHT: Cycling costume in 1894 from Modes d' Alexandre Albert, Paris. OPPOSITE PAGE BOTTOM LEFT: Again Los Angeles model, Dawn Morris, today. (Dwgs. courtesy of the Harper's Bazaar.)

206

THEN & NOW:

OPPOSITE: PAGE TOP: MGM's 1938 adventure motion picture, "Too Hot to Handle," about competing newsreel cameramen. The scene pictured is war-torn China as rival cameramen Clark Gable; Walter Pidgeon; Leo Carrillo et al wait for Japanese planes to attack. After talking the other cameramen into putting their cameras away and call it a day, Gable picks up a hand held motion picture camera, saunters over to an anti-aircraft gun, pulls the lanyard, firing the gun, provoking the high flying aircraft to attack. OPPOSITE PAGE BOTTOM LEFT: Gable films while the planes attack. OPPOSITE PAGE BOTTOM RIGHT: Gable is ecstatic with the pictures he has just taken, scooping the other cameramen. TOP OF PAGE: Gable runs from a whistling bomb that explodes behind him. CENTER OF PAGE: Walter Pidgeon and Leo Carrillo console a muddy Clark Gable. (Photos courtesy of MGM.) BOTTOM OF PAGE: MGM's nostalgia-filled 68-acre back lot is today townhouses and luxury apartments. During the depression, Hollywood's credo was, "Motion Pictures Are Your Best Entertainment," and they truly were. MGM's galaxy of stars reigned supreme and Gable was King. Practically all of MGM's fabulous stars at one time or another had worked on the back lot. From Rudolph Valentino's, "Four Horsemen of the Apocalypse" in 1924 and "Ben Hur" in 1925, on through the advent of the talkies to "That's Entertainment" in the seventies, MGM motion pictures had style, intelligence and most importantly — they entertained. (From the MGM release "TOO HOT TO HANDLE" © 1938 Loew's Incorporated. Ren. 1965 Metro-Goldwyn-Mayer Inc.)

THEN & NOW:

ABOVE LEFT: Warner Bros. gate in 1932. Warner Bros. revolutionized the film industry on October 6, 1927 with the opening of "The Jazz Singer," after acquiring the rights to the Bell Telephone Laboratories system called Vitaphone. Warners also gave the thirties spectacular musicals and action adventure films with James Cagney, Humphrey Bogart and without a doubt the personification of the perfect hero with a sword; in an aircraft; on a horse or in the bedroom: Errol Flynn — he could do it all. (Courtesy of Bison Archives.) ABOVE RIGHT: That same entrance today. Warners today like the rest of the studios distribute many pictures under their name that were actually made by independent producers.

LEFT IN CENTER OF PAGE: The old Paramount gate through which a parade of stars entered the studio: Gary Cooper, Cary Grant, Ronald Colman, Bob Hope, Maurice Chevalier and Bing Crosby to name a few men; Clara Bow, Carole Lombard, Marlene Dietrich and the list goes on and on. Cecil B. de Mille dominated the famous producers and directors of Paramount. (Courtesy of the Bison Archives.) BELOW: The new Paramount gate in Hollywood; the old gate now is used as a back door for foot traffic.

Washington D.C.
The City Freedom Built

THEN & NOW: Above, the White House lawn, Washington D.C. in July, 1911. Harry Atwood taking off in a Wright Type B plane. (Courtesy of the Library of Congress.) Below, Northrop's Mach 2 Tigershark (F20) flies over the Washington Monument, as it concludes an unrefueled, transcontinental flight from California. (Courtesy of Northrop.)

THEN & NOW:

OPPOSITE PAGE TOP: George Washington laying the original cornerstone to the Nation's Capital in Washington D.C. Painting by Clyde De Land. (Courtesy of the Library of Congress.) OPPOSITE PAGE BOTTOM LEFT: The plaque over this actual stone in the Capital. OPPOSITE PAGE BOTTOM RIGHT: The Capital today.

ABOVE: The original Capital in Washington D.C. as completed in 1800. Painting by William R. Birch. (Courtesy of the Library of Congress.) BELOW: The Nation's Capital today. Washington — the city that freedom built was the first national capital planned and built exclusively for its seat of government (others have since). In 1891 Washington directed surveyors to lay out the boundaries. Madison, Jefferson and Washington all favored a site on the Potomac River.

211

THEN & NOW: Above, the Capital of the United States in Washington D.C. Aquatint by Thomas Sutherland after the original watercolor design by Benjamin H. Latiobe. Published by R. Akerman Jan., 1825. The original Capital building on the preceding page is the building on the right. (Courtesy of the Library of Congress.) Below, the Capital Building today.

THEN & NOW: Above, northeast view of the Capital with the new extension in 1852. Engraving by J.S. Steel after T.V. Walter. (Courtesy of the Library of Congress.) Below, the Capital today. The original cornerstone laid by George Washington is located in the archway just behind the man's head in the foreground.

Philadelphia

The Birthplace of a Nation

THEN & NOW:

ABOVE: Philadelphia, Pennsylvania from the Delaware River. The tall steeple on the right is Christ Church and the steeple down Chestnut Street on the left is Independence Hall. Painting by William Nowland Van Powell for the 200th Anniversary (1776 - 1976) of the Declaration of Independence. Courtesy of Holiday Inn, 4th and Arch St., Philadelphia where his original paintings are on exhibit. BELOW: Today. Christ Church on the right; Independence Hall is between the second and third masts on the ship and William Penn atop City Hall is above the aft end of the ship. OPPOSITE PAGE TOP: The Declaration of Independence being approved by the Continental Congress on July 4, 1776 at Independence Hall in Philadelphia, Pennsylvania. This engraving is by Ormsby from the famous painting by John Trumbull. The five men standing to the left of the table are John Adams, Roger Sherman, Robert Livingston, Thomas Jefferson and Benjamin Franklin who said, "Gentlemen, we must all hang together, else we shall all hang separately." OPPOSITE PAGE BOTTOM: Independence Hall today in Philadelphia. The two windows to the right of the white doors are the windows to the actual hall pictured above. That hall today is a National Shrine, with the original furniture and silver inkstand used by these giants of history. (Above photo courtesy of the Library of Congress.)

216

THEN & NOW: ABOVE: Philadelphia, Pennsylvania at the Arch Street waterfront on the Delaware River. From a print dated 1800 by Bingham. (Courtesy of the Free Library of Philadelphia.) BELOW: The Delaware River today. OPPOSITE PAGE TOP: Independence Hall (called the State House then) in 1799. The steeple which had deteriorated had been removed in 1781; the present steeple was erected in 1828. It was here that Thomas Jefferson (1743 - 1826) wrote, "We hold these truths to be self evident that all men are created equal, that they are endowed by their Creator with certain unalienable Rights, that among these are Life, Liberty and the pursuit of Happiness." Engraving by William Russell Birch (1755 - 1834) published in 1800. (Courtesy of the Free Library of Philadelphia.) OPPOSITE PAGE BOTTOM: The exact same location today.

THEN & NOW:

OPPOSITE PAGE TOP: Philadelphia, Pennsylvania at Library Hall in 1799, the home of the Library Company of Philadelphia founded by Benjamin Franklin and his friends in 1731 (the oldest subscription library in the United States). Engraving by William Russell Birch (1755 - 1834) published in 1800. OPPOSITE PAGE BOTTOM: A faithful reconstruction of Library Hall as it appears today. (Dwg. courtesy of the Free Library of Philadelphia.)

ABOVE: Philadelphia, Pennsylvania in the early 19th Century from the Camden side of the Delaware River. The tall steeple in the center is Christ Church where Washington, Franklin and other of the founding fathers worshipped. Aquatint by Garneray. (Courtesy of the Free Library of Philadelphia.) BELOW: Philadelphia today; the white steeple in the center is Christ Church and the steeple between the second and third masts on the ship is Independence Hall.

220

THEN & NOW: ABOVE: Philadelphia, Pennsylvania at the Stratford Hotel on Broad Street in 1895. Congressman, Edward Morrell, is in the driver's seat of the carriage. (Courtesy of the Free Library of Philadelphia.) BELOW: Modern carriages at the Bellevue Stratford Hotel. OPPOSITE PAGE TOP: Independence Hall in Philadelphia in 1876; celebrating the 100th Anniversary of the Declaration of Independence. From a lithograph by Thomas Hunter. (Courtesy of the Free Library of Philadelphia.) OPPOSITE PAGE BOTTOM: The same scene today.

THEN & NOW:

Below, the 37 foot tall, 30 ton statue of William Penn (1644 - 1718) prior to it being hoisted to the top of Philadelphia's City Hall which was completed in 1901. William Penn founded three American colonies — Pennsylvania, New Jersey and Delaware. He also named Philadelphia (the City of Brotherly Love) and instructed the surveyors on the layout of the city, reserving spaces for markets and parks. (Courtesy of the Library of Philadelphia.) Above, City Hall today.

THEN & NOW: Above, Philadelphia, Pennsylvania at Broad and Market Streets in 1800. The Water Works or Pump House was out in the suburbs. Engraving by William Russell Birch (1755 - 1834) published in 1800. Below, today at that exact location is Philadelphia's City Hall — in the dead center of metropolitan Philadelphia. (Dwg. courtesy of the Free Library of Philadelphia.)

New York

From the Bowery to the Glittering Palaces of Glass and Steel

THEN & NOW: Above, "View of Brooklyn L.I. from the U.S. Hotel New York," was the title of this lithograph by E. Whitefield — printed by F. Michelin in the middle of the 19th Century. (Courtesy of the Library of Congress.) Below, the same view today from the top of the World Trade Center.

THEN & NOW:

ABOVE: The Statue of Liberty looms over a Paris street in 1884 as it nears completion in Frederic Auguste Bartholdi's (1834 - 1904) courtyard. (Courtesy of the National Archives.) BELOW: The colossal godlike statue towers over New York Harbor. Dedicated in 1886, the observation platform in Liberty's crown is 260 feet above the harbor's surface. The glorious sight of this lovely lady at twilight from the deck of a Liberty Ship, returning from World War II, was an unforgettable, emotional experience for this writer, as it has also been for millions of other men, women and children coming to America. (Courtesy of the National Park Service.)

On a plaque in the pedestal
Emma Lazarus' poem reads:

*". . . Give me your tired,
        your poor
Your huddled masses
        yearning to breathe free,
The wretched refuse
        of your teeming shore.
Send these, the homeless,
        tempest-tossed to me
I lift my lamp
        beside the golden door!"*

THEN & NOW: Above, looking north from North Dutch Church in 1845. The building with the tower in the center is the New York City Hall, built in 1812. Below, today that same City Hall building is surrounded by high-rise office building. (Above — Courtesy of the National Archives.)

THEN & NOW:

Above, New York's Forty Second Street in 1891, the steepled building in the center is Grand Central Station. (Courtesy of the New York Public Library.) Below, mighty Grand Central Station, the nerve center of the bustling metropolis, is that cramped white building in the center of the picture, dwarfed by the Chrysler Building and others in this man-made canyon.

227

THEN & NOW: Above, New York's Fifth Avenue at 48th Street in 1894 brings back memories of things past — e.g., Irving Berlin's masterpiece: "On Fifth Ave... In your Easter bonnet, with all the frills upon it, you'll be the grandest lady in the Easter Parade... the photographers will snap us and you'll find that you're in the Rotogravure... On Fifth Avenue... Fifth Avenue..." Below, Fifth Avenue at 48th, today. (Above — Courtesy of the National Archives.)

THEN & NOW: Above, "The Great East River Suspension Bridge," was the title of this Currier and Ives Lithograph. (Courtesy of the Library of Congress.) The dedication on May 24, 1883 was attended by President Chester A. Arthur. It was the largest suspension bridge in the world, connecting Manhattan and Brooklyn. Father and son, engineering geniuses, the Roeblings, were pioneer builders of big suspension bridges, including the Brooklyn Bridge. Like a Gothic Cathedral in the sky, it is a symbol of the century past. Below, the Brooklyn Bridge (right) a hundred years later is dwarfed as seen from the top of the World Trade Center.

229

THEN & NOW:

Below, Saint Patrick's Cathedral in 1894 with a horse-drawn bus going down Fifth Avenue. Above, the same location today. (Below — Courtesy of the National Archives.)

THEN & NOW: Above, New York City 1849, "drawn from nature and on stone," by C. Bachmann. Lithograph of Sarony and Major. (Courtesy of the Library of Congress.) Below, the same view from the top of the Empire State Building. The bridges over the East River can be seen to the left. The Twin World Trade Center is in the center and the Statue of Liberty to the right of the Center.

231

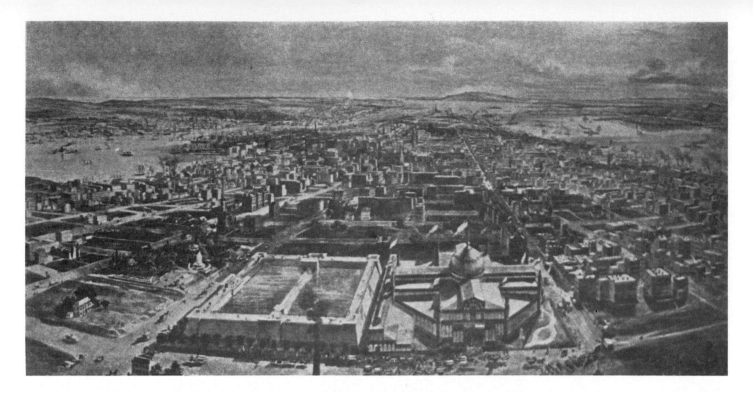

THEN & NOW: Above, New York City in the 19th Century. (Courtesy of the National Archives.) Below, the same scene today as seen from the top of the Rockefeller Center with the Empire State Building in the center, the Twin World Trade Center behind and to the right and a tiny Statue of Liberty in the middle of the Hudson River. The Empire State Building, built in 1931 was the tallest building in the world (1,250 feet) for over 40 years; until the Twin World Trade Center (1,350 feet) was completed in 1972. However, the title was turned over to Chicago, Illinois on May 4, 1973 with the completion of the 1,454 feet Sear's Tower.

232

The Sea

233

THEN & NOW:

ABOVE: The Confederate Submarine "H.L. Hunley" on December 6, 1863 at Charleston, South Carolina. On February 17, 1864, the "Hunley" sank the "USS Housatonic" which was blockading Charleston. This was a historic first, at a horrific price — the explosion also sank the "Hunley." The problem was the propulsion system — men cranking a gear manually was an inefficient way to turn the propeller at a top speed of 4 knots. BELOW: The U.S. Navy's nuclear powered attack submarine "Skipjack" with a top submerged speed of 40 miles per hour. The attack submarine's primary mission is the destruction of enemy submarines by launching a missle horizontally from the torpedo tubes; away from the ship a rocket motor ignites; then the missle rises vertically out of the water; a guidance system takes it to the target; the missle re-enters the water at supersonic speed and the nuclear warhead explodes, destroying the enemy submarine. The "Skipjack's" secondary mission is to provide a principal part of the America's deterrent to nuclear war; being able to launch 2,500 mile missles with nuclear warheads deep into the heartland of any nation on earth. These submarines can preserve freedom and maintain the peace. (Photos courtesy of the U.S. Navy.)

THEN & NOW:

ABOVE: Eugene Ely taking off the converted deck of the "USS Pennsylvania" in his Curtis Biplane in 1911. BELOW: The U.S. Navy's nuclear-powered "Enterprise" with men in formation forming the letters $E = MC^2$ on the 4½ acre flight deck, which is 123 feet above the water. She is 1,123 feet long, with a crew of 5,000 and 14,000 meals are served daily. Eight nuclear reactors give her the tremendous speed of 35½ knots (40 miles an hour). A moving 90,000 ton city with 3,200 rooms. She is the home of Mach 2.6 fighters; nuclear attack aircraft; helicopters; rockets; missiles and 1,000 pound bombs guided to their target by gyrostabilized television cameras. The two other nuclear-powered ships are the Cruiser "Long Beach" and the Frigate "Bainbridge." (Photos courtesy of the U.S. Navy.) OPPOSITE PAGE TOP: The American Continental Navy Frigate Hancock (the fastest sailer of the world) gives the morning gun salute during the Revolutionary War. Painting by William Nowland Van Powell and courtesy of Holiday Inn - Philadelphia. OPPOSITE PAGE BOTTOM: The USS Battleship "Iowa" off Pearl Harbor. (Courtesy of the U.S. Navy.)

234

THEN & NOW:

ABOVE: The first United States Naval Task Force raid, under Commodore Hopkins, during the Revolutionary War. Painting by William Nowland Van Powell — Courtesy of Holiday Inn - Philadelphia. BELOW: A rare photograph which shows all the "Iowa-Class" Battleships steaming in formation. From the foreground the "Iowa; "Wisconsin"; "Missouri" and "New Jersey." Without question the "Iowa-Class" Battleships were the best ever built; they possessed high speed, good protection and great offensive power. The "New Jersey" and the "Missouri" have been refurbished. (Photo courtesy of the U.S. Navy.) OPPOSITE PAGE TOP: During the Revolutionary War, the American Continental Navy Brig Reprisal being chased by the British Seventy Four Gun Burford. Painting by William Nowland Van Powell — Courtesy of the Holiday Inn - Philadelphia. OPPOSITE PAGE BOTTOM: The USS Battleship "Missouri." A full broadside from her 16 inch guns weighs over 12 tons. (Photo courtesy of the U.S. Navy.)

236

238

THEN & NOW:

ABOVE: The American Frigate Randolph, in a broadside battle with the sixty-four gun British Yarmouth during the Revolutionary War. Painting by William Nowland Van Powell and courtesy of Holiday Inn - Philadelphia. BELOW: The USS Battleship "New Jersey" firing a broadside at night. During 47 days at sea in the Vietnam War she fired 5,688 rounds of 16 inch shells and more than 15,000 5 inch shells. During World War II, the "New Jersey" sunk the Japanese cruiser "Katori" and the destroyer "Maikaze" at Eniwetok Atoll. And Admiral Halsey commanded the Fleet from the "New Jersey" during the Luzon Campaign. (Courtesy of the U.S. Navy.)

THEN & NOW:

Above, the American Frigate "Randolph" explodes in combat with the British "Yarmouth" during the Revolutionary War. Painting by William Nowland Van Powell for the 200th Anniversary (1776 - 1976) of the Declaration of Independence. Courtesy of Holiday Inn, 4th and Arch St., Philadelphia, PA where his original paintings are on exhibit. Below, the "Bikini Atomic Bomb Test" of July 25, 1946. An August, 1946 Life Magazine stated, "...It was perhaps the most awesome man-made spectacle ever photographed... The bomb was suspended in a concrete caisson below a landing ship... a solid pilar of water climbed 5,500 feet." The dark spot in the right side of the column is the battleship "Arkansas" going up; sinking before the cloud cleared away. The old carrier "Saratoga" sank in eight hours and the Japanese battleship "Nagato" also sank. Other sinking ships were beached so their damage could be studied. On March 1, 1954 the explosion of a Hydrogen Bomb caused an island in the Pacific to disappear, leaving a hole 175 feet deep and a mile in diameter. Today one bomb is capable of devastating 150 square miles. Lord help us. (Courtesy of the Library of Congress.)

239

Air and Space

From Kitty Hawk to the Moon.

THEN & NOW:

OPPOSITE PAGE TOP: The world's first powered, sustained and controlled flight on December 17, 1903 by Orville Wright at Kitty Hawk, North Carolina. BELOW: July 21, 1969 — the first man on the Moon on the Sea of Tranquility. Neil Armstrong was first, followed by Edwin Aldrin while Michael Collins parked in Moon orbit in the Command Module. After a stay of 21 hours and 36 minutes the Eagle lifted off the Moon and returned to the Command Module. With 48.5 lbs. of Moon rocks, Apollo 11 blasted out of Lunar orbit, for their ecstatic return to Mother Earth. On July 24, 1969 they made a safe parachuting splash down in the Pacific Ocean, 11 miles from their recovery ship, the U.S.S. Hornet; thus completing the most historic event in 2,000 years. The mural of the Astronaut and flag on the OPPOSITE PAGE BELOW covers a massive wall at the National Air and Space Museum in Washington D.C. (Photos courtesy of the National Air and Space Museum.) ABOVE: The Martin NBS-1 Bomber had a top speed of 98 mph in 1920 with an absolute ceiling of 10,000 feet. BELOW: The Rockwell International B-1 Strategic Bomber that has been clocked at Mach 2 (twice the speed of sound.) The B-1 can carry 12½ tons of nuclear or conventional weapons. (Photos courtesy of the National Air and Space Museum.)

242

THEN & NOW: OPPOSITE PAGE TOP: The Wright brother's plane thrills the crowd in 1908. OPPOSITE PAGE BOTTOM: Charles A. Lindbergh's, "Spirit of St. Louis" (Ryan Aircraft.) In May 1927, Lindbergh became the symbol of heroism by making a solo 33½ hour, 3,610 mile flight from New York to Paris. ABOVE: April 12, 1981, the Space Shuttle, Columbia, with Astronauts, John Young and Robert Crippen, lifts off the pad at the Kennedy Space Center in Florida. After 54 hours in orbit, the Columbia completed the first historic flight of a Space Shuttle ending with an unpowered landing at Edward's Air Force Base in California, witnessed by untold millions of people at the site and on television all over the world. This was the first return from space without using parachutes. Proving its reliability, the Space Shuttle repeated its achievement and by July 4, 1982 the "Columbia" had flown five successful missions. (Opposite page photos courtesy of the National Air and Space Museum and above photo courtesy of NASA.)

THEN & NOW:

ABOVE: George Eastman (1854 - 1932) aboard the S.S. Gallia in 1890 with his $1 Pocket Kodak Brownie camera being photographed with a similar camera by Fred Church. Eastman invented and manufactured photographic materials and cameras. The Kodak Brownie went on sale in 1888. He had a virtual monopoly in the United States. A great humanitarian and philanthropist, he gave away $75,000,000 in his lifetime. (Photo courtesy of the National Archives.) BELOW: A fantastic view of the Earth as photographed from the Apollo 17. This outstanding photograph extends from the Mediterranean Sea to the Antarctica south polar ice caps. Almost the entire coastline of the continent of Africa is clearly defined. The Arabian peninsula can be seen at the northeastern edge of Africa; Asia is on the horizon toward the northeast. (Photo courtesy of NASA.)

OPPOSITE PAGE TOP: Columbus landing in America on October 12, 1492. Painting by John Vanderlyn (1775 - 1852).(Courtesy of the Library of Congress.) OPPOSITE PAGE BOTTOM: Man's first landing on the Moon on July 21, 1969 witnessed live on radio and television by more than a billion people all over the world. Astronaut, Edwin Aldrin, poses by the American Flag for Neil Armstrong's 70mm lunar surface camera. Because of Columbus, one date in the fifteenth century stands out about all others: 1492. A thousand years from today, one date will stand out above all others in the twentieth century: 1969, the year that Neil Armstrong first set foot on the Moon. (Courtesy of NASA.)

245

THEN & NOW: OPPOSITE PAGE TOP: Eugene Ely flying his Curtis Biplane made the first landing on a ship on January 18, 1911; on the converted deck of the U.S.S. Pennsylvania in San Francisco Bay. The sailors on the masts knew they were witnessing history in the making. OPPOSITE PAGE BOTTOM: Catapult launching today. ABOVE: Newsmen witnessing Ely's take off from the deck. BELOW: A double catapult launching today. (Photos courtesy of the U.S. Navy.)

THEN & NOW:

RIGHT: Oldsmobile driven by Lester Whitman and Eugene Hammond from coast to coast. The rear wheels were wet in the Pacific Ocean at San Francisco on July 6, 1903 and the front wheels are shown resting in the Atlantic Ocean on September 22, 1903. BELOW: An artist's concept of the Lunar Roving Vehicle (LRV). (Above photo courtesy of the National Archives; below, courtesy of NASA.)

THEN & NOW:

OPPOSITE PAGE TOP: Henry Ford (1863 - 1947) in 1918 poses in his first car which was built in 1896. Ford is credited with the innovation of the assembly-line for automobile production and the creator of modern mass production. In 1914 when the average worker was making $11 a week, every Ford worker received a minimum of $5 a day. By 1927 15,000,000 Model T's had been built. The Ford Foundation has given more than $2,000,000,000 to educational and social programs. OPPOSITE PAGE BOTTOM: The Lunar Roving Vehicle (LRV) of Apollo 17 on the Moon in December 1972. While Eugene Cernan remained in Lunar orbit, Ronald Evans and Harrison Schmitt landed on the moon in a narrow valley near the southeast rim of the Sea of Serenity. They spent 75 hours exploring the Tauris-Littrow mountainous region of the Moon. On December 14 they rejoined Evans with 249 lbs. of Moon rock and on December 19 they made a successful parachuting splashdown in the Pacific. (Above photo courtesy of the Library of Congress; below, courtesy of NASA.)

THEN & NOW:

ABOVE: The 1912 Curtis Biplane, with a speed of 55 mph. BELOW: The Lockheed Blackbird is a Mach 3 aircraft, with speed up to 2,193 mph, it has reached 85,069 feet. It has flown from New York to London in the transatlantic record of 1 hour, 55 minutes and 32 seconds. (Photos courtesy of the National Air and Space Museum.)

OPPOSITE PAGE TOP: The 1912 Curtis Biplane, with a speed of 55 miles per hour. OPPOSITE PAGE BOTTOM: The North American rocket powered X15 which established a world speed record of 4,534 mph (Mach 6.72) and it climbed to a height of 354,200 feet (67.08 miles). (Photos courtesy of the National Air and Space Museum.)

THEN & NOW:

Above left, Charles Lindbergh (1902 - 1974) ready to fly. The "Lone Eagle" made the first solo flight between New York and Paris in 1927. As an airmail pilot he heard about the $25,000 prize offered by Raymond Ortega, a New York hotel owner for the first nonstop flight between New York and Paris. Backed by St. Louis businessmen, Lindbergh supervised the construction of "The Spirit of St. Louis" at the Ryan Company in San Diego. He flew it to New York in record time and on the foggy, rainy morning of May 20, 1927 he left Roosevelt Field, Long Island, touching down 33½ hours later at Paris, France and a legend was born. (Courtesy of the National Air and Space Museum.)

Above right, Neil Armstrong (born 1930) ready to rocket to the Moon. Armstrong was the first man to set foot on the Moon — a mere 42 years after Lindbergh's epic flight. History had taken a quantum leap. A graduate aeronautical engineer and a test pilot, Neil Armstrong flew 78 combat missions as a Navy pilot in the Korean War. He flew the rocket-driven X-15. With David Scott in the Gemini 8 spacecraft, they completed the first successful docking of two spaceships in March, 1966. On July 20, 1969 Neil Armstrong stepped off Apollo 11's footpad onto the mysterious surface of the Moon and spoke those famous words, "That's one small step for man, one giant leap for mankind." (Courtesy of NASA.)

THEN & NOW:

ABOVE: The driving of the "Golden Spike", the most famous photograph of the 19th Century, taken by Andrew J. Russell on May 10, 1869 with the dramatic meeting of the Central Pacific building from the west and Union Pacific from the east at Promontory, Utah, completing the first transcontinental railroad. BELOW: On April 14, 1981, "Columbia" the world's first space shuttle touches down at Edward's Air Force Base in California. Piloted by 50 year old John Young, who commanded Apollo 16 when it landed on the Moon, along with Bob Crippen, 43, they had launched at Cape Canaveral, Florida and orbited the Earth 36 times. Coming down from orbit, the "Columbia" crossed the California coast near Big Sur at Mach 7, seven times the speed of sound or about 5,100 mph. Finally at Edwards AFB, now flying as a 102 ton glider, they brought the "Columbia" down, witnessed by untold millions on TV all over the world. (Top photo from the National Archives; bottom courtesy of NASA.)

Index

Luxor Temple—Egypt